100 FREEMASONS

In Freemasonry, the supremacy of the spirit manifests itself in the strength of the belief in a possible better humanity, occurring through the improvement of all its members.

Irène Mainguyi

KLAUS DĄBROWSKI, 33°
Sovereign Grand Commander
of the Supreme Council of Poland

100 FREEMASONS

1st edition, 6023 A∴L∴

100 Freemasons

Text: Klaus Dąbrowski

Illustrations: (with the use of AI tools): Max Bojarski

Copyright © EDUVOLUTION, 2023

ISBN: 9798389858473

More information: https://freemasonry.network/100-freemasons/

Contact: admin@freemasonry.network

TABLE OF CONTENTS

AUTHORS' INTRODUCTION

SEEKERS OF LIGHT*

B∴ Klaus Dąbrowski

March 3, 6023 A∴L∴

Freemasonry is an ancient and universal spiritual tradition that unites people of different nationalities, worldviews, and professions in search of truth and brotherhood. Its history is rich and complex, full of inspiration and thought-provoking. Among its members were great thinkers, artists, leaders, and heroes who influenced the formation of civilization.

This book presents the profiles of one hundred prominent Freemasons from different eras and countries whose activities contributed to the development of mankind. They are not the only or most important Freemasons in history, but from their example, one can try to assess what Freemasonry is able to offer the world.

Some of them are well-known and widely respected, while others are little known or forgotten. Some were saints or martyrs to their cause; others were sinners or rebels. Some were conservatives or reformers; others were revolutionaries or utopians. Some were philosophers or poets; others were scientists or inventors. Some were politicians or military men, while others were humanists or philanthropists.

However, all of them (with a few exceptions that seem to prove the rule, such as Tsar Alexander I or Kaiser Wilhelm I, who, having joined the Freemasonry, did not get rid of their authoritarian inclinations; moreover, over time, for both of them, affiliation became "uncomfortable") shared similar values: they had the courage to seek the Light in the darkness of ignorance and fanaticism; they had the passion for learning about themselves and the world; they shared freedom of thought and action; they were true to their ideals; they hoped for a better future for humanity.

At the same time, it is worth remembering an important principle: it is not Freemasonry that acts outwardly, but individual Freemasons. Freemasonry inspires within its lodges, and what each individual adept will do with this inspiration when he leaves the temple is a matter of his own conscience; in Freemasonry, no one can order him to do anything. Nevertheless, it turns out that all these, often so different, people do indeed have something in common.

This book is neither an apologia nor a criticism of Freemasonry. It is an attempt to show its beauty and power through the lives of its chosen representatives. It is an invitation to discover this fascinating spiritual tradition from your own point of view.

Let this book be a source of inspiration and reflection for you on what it means to be a Freemason - not just a member of an organization or a participant in a ritual - but above all, a Man seeking the Light.

∴

---

* „Seekers of Light" is the title of a book by Maciej B.Stępień, a Catholic researcher, who presented in it a very objective picture of Freemasonry. I read it more than twenty-one years ago, and it brought me the final arguments for joining Freemasonry. I applied and was accepted.

HOW WAS THIS BOOK COMPOSED

All of the portraits of famous Freemasons and all of the illustrations featured on the odd pages were created thanks to AI (artificial intelligence) tools. The creation of a work of art, such as a portrait, requires issuing appropriate, sufficiently precise commands to artificial intelligence, so the role of humans cannot be overestimated, while the computer still remains a creative tool in the process.

The illustrations on the odd pages are usually loose artistic "variations on a theme" of some thread in the life of a given character rather than historically faithful illustrations of a given event.

The individual figures are listed chronologically, according to their date of death (this is a logical arrangement insofar as most often people mentioned in this book were active until the very end of their lives, usually more so when they were elderly than in their youth).

At the same time, famous individual Freemasons were assigned to eight categories (each corresponds to a different background color of the book's text), as illustrated on the next page. Sometimes, when a figure would fit into more than one category, an arbitrary choice had to be made.

Philosophers:

Artists:

Rulers - Kings and Emperors:

Politicians - Statesmen:

Scientists, Inventors and Entrepreneurs:

Commanders:

Social activists:

Adventurers, Sportsmen:

100 FREEMASONS

JOHN LOCKE

*The end of law is not to abolish or restrain
but to preserve and enlarge freedom.*

John Locke

John Locke (1632-1704) was an English
political philosopher, economist, and physician. He created a classical form of empiri-
cism and liberalism and a theory of the
value of money (monetarism). He made his
mark in world history, especially with his
theories on individual liberty and government based on the social contract. Locke
believed that the main purpose of government, operating under the social contract,
should be the protection of individual
rights, including liberty and private property. These theories were important to the
development of political thought and philosophy in the 17th and 18th centuries, were
eventually adapted by many countries, and
formed the basis for modern democracy and the rule of law. Locke was one of the main
founders of liberal philosophy. Some of his works were included in the papal index of
banned books.

According to C. Lenning's "Encyclopedia of Freemasonry," Locke was admitted to the
lodge in 1696, which was 20 years before the beginning of organized Freemasonry.
Admittedly, there is nonetheless debate as to his affiliation, but given that there is
a letter in which he admits it and that many of his Freemason contemporaries considered
him a Brother, we think we can include him in this book.

JONATHAN SWIFT

Satire is a sort of glass wherein beholders do generally discover everybody's face but their own.

Jonathan Swift

Jonathan Swift (1667-1745) was an Irish writer and satirist. He is known as the author of "Gulliver's Travels," one of the most important books of the English Enlightenment. Swift was a political writer, and in his works, he criticized the society of his era, using irony, humor, and fantasy.
He spent a third of his income on charity.
His influence on literature and culture is undeniable. He inspired many writers, such as George Orwell and Lewis Carroll. His works are still read and appreciated by modern readers around the world.

Swift belonged to the 'Goat-at-the-Foot-of-the-Haymarket, № 16' lodge in London.

MONTESQUIEU

There is no greater tyranny than that which is perpetrated under the shield of the law and in the name of justice.

Montesquieu, "The Spirit of the Laws. "

Montesquieu (1689-1755) was a French philosopher and writer whose main contribution to world history lies in his formulation of the theory of democracy. His most important book, "The Spirit of the Laws," published in 1748, was an important voice in the debate on the nature of power and its limits, ending up on the papal index of banned books. Montesquieu argued that power should be divided into three independent parts – the legislature, the executive, and the judiciary – a principle of tri-partition that is considered crucial to the functioning of democracy and individual rights. Montesquieu's views inspired many countries in the process of building democratic systems.

He became a Freemason probably in 1729 at 'Horn Tavern Lodge' in Westminster. He helped establish a lodge in the 'Rue de Bussy' in 1735. Reports on the work of the Grand Lodge founded in 1717 show that he attended its meetings around 1738 and met with such "classics" of Freemasonry as John Theophilus Desaguliers and James Anderson.

FRANCIS I, HOLY ROMAN EMPEROR

The power of the Habsburgs is not, as in the case of other dynasties,
tied to a specific country or countries - because the mission,
tied to the family name, does not cease with the loss of a country,
and is not exhausted with the possession of a single crown,
but is subject to its own law.

Emil Franzel, "The Habsburgs."

Francis I, Holy Roman Emperor (1745-1765), also known as Franz I of Habsburg, was the ruler of Austria and King of Germany from 1745 to 1765. He is considered one of the most important rulers in the history of the Habsburgs, who reigned in Europe for more than four hundred years. His main contribution to world history was the significant strengthening of the family's position in Europe and the introduction of political and economic reforms that contributed to the development and modernization of the state. Francis, I was also a significant patron of art and culture, which influenced the flourishing of the Baroque in Austria. He amassed many valuable works of art, including paintings, sculptures, and manuscripts, in palaces and residences that he owned. In his political and cultural activities, Francis I laid a solid foundation for the further development and expansion of the Habsburg Empire.

He was initiated in 1731 into the Grand Lodge of England by John Theophilus Desaguliers at a lodge specially established for the purpose in The Hague, in the home of the British ambassador. Later, on a visit to England, he was elevated to the rank of Master Mason at a lodge (also created just for the occasion) at Houghton Hall (Norfolk), the estate of British Prime Minister Robert Walpole.

HELVETIUS

Truth is the torch that gleams through the fog without dispelling it.

Claude Adrien Helvétius

Claude Adrien Helvétius (1715-1771), a French philosopher and economist, made a significant contribution to world history with his views on education and human nature. He reiterated, following Lock, that the mind has no innate ideas, and that man is born as a blank tablet, or "tabula rasa," and therefore, education plays a key role. In this regard, he promoted the idea of equality and equal opportunities for all people. He claimed that selfishness was the driving force behind human actions, criticized morality based on religion, and introduced the concept of utilitarianism into philosophy and economics. He expounded the principles of his philosophy in his book "On the Mind" ("De l'esprit"), which provoked fierce opposition from the Church and university authorities and was publicly burned. At the same time, it was welcomed by Enlightenment circles, and Helvetius was eagerly invited by them to discuss it (for example, in 1765, he visited Prussia at the personal invitation of Frederick II). Helvétius was one of the most important philosophers of the 18th century, and his views had a significant impact on the development of philosophy, economics, and political theory.

Helvétius was a member of the famous Lodge of the Nine Sisters (La Loge des Neuf Sœurs) in Paris, which also included Voltaire, Franklin, and Jacques Montgolfier, among others.

VOLTAIRE

I disapprove of what you say, but I will defend to the death your right to say it.

(Summary of Voltaire's views on freedom of speech by English writer Evelyn Beatrice Hall)

Voltaire (1694-1778) was a French philosopher, writer, and publicist. His main contribution to world history was his fight for human rights, including freedom of speech, thought, and conscience. His works are full of satire and criticism of certain aspects of society and institutions, such as the church, the state apparatus, and the monarchy. Voltaire was also an outspoken opponent of intolerance and discrimination, including anti-Semitism and racism. His philosophy and views had a significant impact on the development of Enlightenment thought and inspired the French Revolution, although he treated any ideology with reserve. Voltaire is  also considered one of the most important French writers of his time, and his works, such as "Candide," are considered classics of French literature.

In 1778, Voltaire met Ben Franklin at the Academy of Sciences (who by then had seniority of 40 years in Freemasonry), who invited him to join the Paris lodge of the 'Nine Sisters.' The membership of Voltaire, who became a Freemason shortly before his death, was already an icon of the Enlightenment and was representative of Masonic ideals.

LESSING

The worst superstition is
to consider our own tolerable.

Gotthold Ephraim Lessing

Gotthold Ephraim Lessing (1729-1781) was a German playwright, theater reformer, philosopher, and literary critic. His main contribution to world history was the promotion of rationalism and religious tolerance. In his dramatic and philosophical works, Lessing, inspired by Voltaire, argued for freedom of speech and thought, as well as the equality of all religions. He recognized the right of everyone to seek truth and the path to salvation on his own. He identified happiness and freedom with the attainment of spiritual maturity associated with the rejection of superstition. His works, such as "Nathan der Weise" ("Natan the Sage") and "Minna von Barnhelm" ("Minna of Barnhelm"), demonstrate his philosophy of religious tolerance and equality of all people. Lessing also made significant contributions to the development of theater and drama theory, and his ideas about these fields were put into practice by subsequent generations of playwrights and directors. Lessing's works contributed to the development of critical and scientific thought, and his legacy is still relevant to modern culture and philosophy.

October 14, 1771, Lessing was initiated at the lodge 'Zu den drei Goldenen Rosen' ('Under the three golden roses') in Hamburg.

JOHANN CHRISTIAN BACH

I was obliged to be industrious. Whoever is equally industrious will succeed equally well.

Johann Christian Bach

Johann Christian Bach (1735-1782) was one of the most versatile composers of the second half of the 18th century. The youngest of Johann Sebastian Bach's four sons (all of whom were talented musicians). Known as the "Milanese" or "London Bach," he was a cathedral organist in Milan in 1760 and concertmaster to Queen Sophie Charlotte in London in 1762. He composed operas, arias, cantatas, chamber music, symphonies, and overtures. His style of music, often described as gallant, is characterized by graceful melodicism, an excellent sense of form, and ingenuity in the use of orchestral texture and color. He had a significant influence on the music of Wolfgang Amadeus Mozart.

He was an early member of the 'Lodge of Nine Muses № 235' working in London.

FREDERICK II THE GREAT

The greatest and noblest pleasure
which we have in this world
is to discover new truths,
and the next is to shake off old prejudices.

Frederick II the Great

Frederick II the Great (1712-1786), King of Prussia from 1740 to 1786, made significant contributions to world history through his reforms and actions on the international stage. Under his rule, Prussia became one of the most powerful European states. His main achievements were:
- Internal reforms: Frederick the Great introduced many internal reforms that streamlined and modernized state and economic administration. In particular, he established a new judicial and administrative system that ensured a fairer and more efficient justice system.
- Enlightened rule: Frederick the Great was a supporter of the Enlightenment, and his rule was dominated by the philosophy of this movement. He introduced many educational and cultural reforms that increased the level of knowledge and culture in the country.
- Military activities: Frederick the Great was known for waging wars, including the Seven Years' War, which marked the beginning of Prussia's development as a military and political power in Europe.
- Influence on philosophy and culture: Frederick the Great was also a patron of the arts and literature, and his kingdom was home to many outstanding artists and intellectuals.
He introduced many cultural reforms. These and other activities of Frederick the Great allowed him to leave a lasting mark on the history of the world and make him one of the most important rulers of his time.

He belonged to Freemasonry since he was initiated in 1738 at an inn in Brunswick. He approved the existence of Freemasonry in Prussia with special patents in 1774. A participant in the work of the 'Rhenisberg' lodge. Patron of the Ancient and Accepted Scottish Rite.

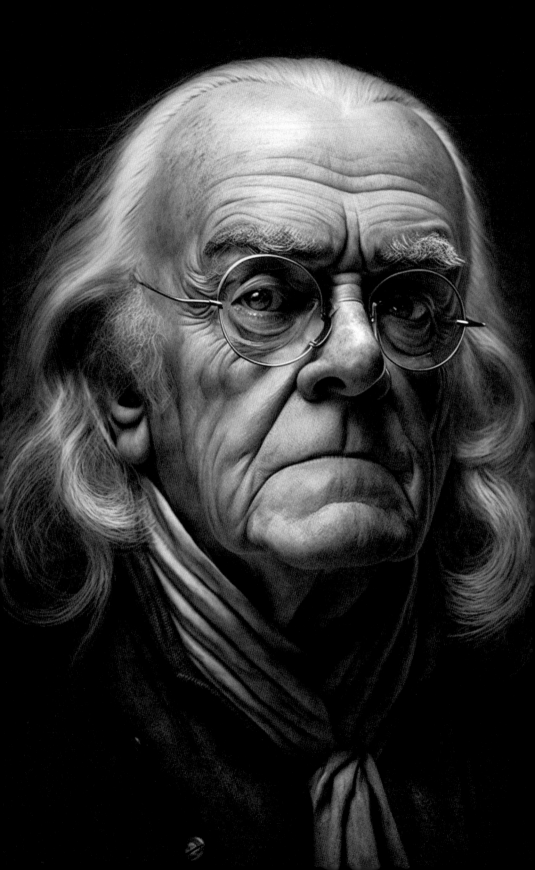

BENJAMIN FRANKLIN

*Any society that would give up
a little liberty to gain a little security
will deserve neither and lose both.*

Benjamin Franklin

Benjamin Franklin (1706-1790) was a politician, philosopher, scientist, and inventor.
Having left his original contributions in
each of these fields, he is regarded as one of
the most versatile, gifted figures in history.
Among other things, he invented bifocal
glasses and the lightning rod. He discovered
and described the Gulf Stream. He co-
founded the first Mutual Assurance fund,
established the first public library in the
United States, and created the academy
known today as the University of Pennsyl-
vania. He was one of the founding fathers
of the United States, co-writing and signing
the Declaration of Independence, worked on
the US Constitution, then served as ambas-

sador to Paris, where he was instrumental in obtaining French assistance in the US struggle
against Great Britain. Franklin successfully promoted ethical development, compiling such
publications as "Poor Richard's Almanack," a popular calendar in which he included maxims,
poems, and advice for each day of the year. Toward the end of his life, he became involved
in the campaign to abolish slavery.

Franklin was initiated in 1731, probably at the February meeting of the 'St. John's Lodge'
in Philadelphia. The respect in which he was held is evidenced by the fact that just a
few years later, in 1735, he was elected Grand Master. As Grand Master, he laid the
cornerstone of Independence Hall in Philadelphia. He was the Worshipful Master of the
Lodge 'Les Neuf Soeurs' (The Nine Sisters) in Paris. In this lodge, he enlisted French
support for the cause of US independence. Franklin lived to the age of eighty-five, sixty of
those years lived as a Freemason: he lived, wrote, and practiced the principles of the Craft.

MOZART

I pay no attention whatsoever to anybody's
praise or blame. I simply follow my own feelings.

Wolfgang Amadeus Mozart

Wolfgang Amadeus Mozart (1756-1791) was one of the greatest composers of all time. He gave concerts as young as five years old. As a child prodigy, he gained fame throughout Europe. Even as an adult, during a tour of Italy, he wrote from memory Allegri's "Miserere" (1770), which, becoming further evidence of his genius, contributed to the legend surrounding his figure. Upon his return in 1772, he became concertmaster at the court of Joseph II. Over the years, Mozart grew increasingly tired of the rigid corset of professional relationships and dependence on an individual employer. He eventually decided to function as an independent artist. His main contri-  bution to the history of the world was the creation of many brilliant musical works that set new standards in the field of music composition and interpretation. Works such as "Don Giovanni," "The magic flute," and "Requiem" are considered milestones in the history of music and continue to be performed and appreciated around the world.

He was an active Freemason (initiated in 1784 at the 'Benevolence' Lodge in Vienna) and created several compositions for his lodge. His opera "The Magic Flute" is full of Masonic references.

ROBERT BURNS

*Man's inhumanity to man makes
countless thousands mourn!*

Robert Burns

Robert Burns (1759-1796) was a poet and composer considered one of the most important representatives of Scottish culture. He showed in poetry the beauty and values of folk culture and extolled family happiness and the charms of a simple life. Burns wrote about his experiences and feelings, as well as about the lives of people from the lower social strata, which was rare in the poetry of the time. His poems were full of emotion, devoid of excessive solemnity and exaltation, instead revealing deeper truths from the daily lives of simple people. Burns' poetry had a clear social dimension, showing

the problems and inequalities in society. Burns also contributed much to musical culture, as his poetry was often sung and played on the guitar. Many of his works became traditional Scottish songs, including "Auld Lang Syne" and "Scots Wha Hae." In this way, Burns contributed to the development of Scotland's national culture and identity. At the same time, he was committed to promoting progressive ideas. The motto of his work was the Latin maxim "Amor vincit omnia" ("Love conquers all").

Burns was initiated on July 4, 1781, at 'St David's Lodge, № 174', in Tarbolton. In October of the same year, he attained the second and third degrees in that lodge. Thereafter he was, until his death, a very active Freemason, also in other lodges and higher degree structures.

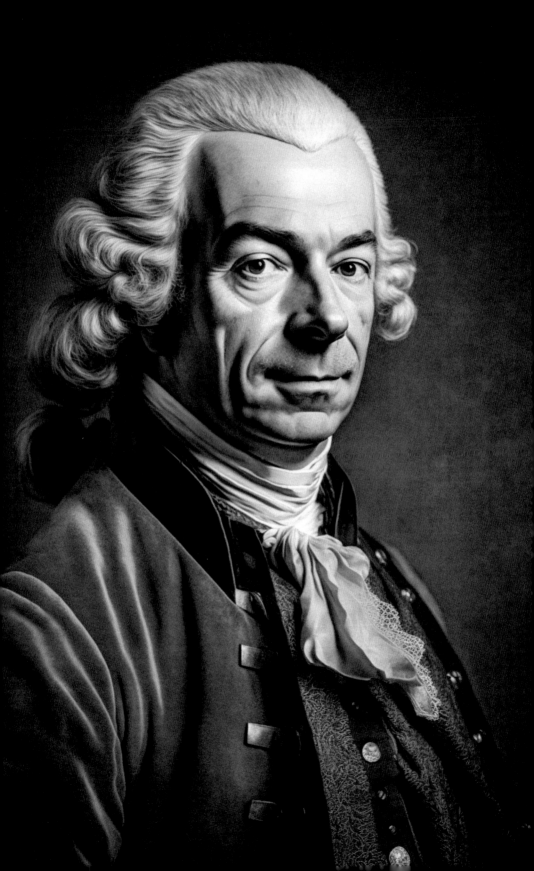

JACQUES MONTGOLFIER

Sic Itur Ad Astra (So, we aim for the stars)

Motto from the family coat of arms of Jacques Étienne Montgolfier,
given by Louis XVI (December 1783) to Pierre Montgolfier
in recognition of his sons' successful balloon flight.

Jacques Étienne Montgolfier is considered one of the fathers of aviation, and his main contribution to world history is the invention and development of the first flying air balloon. In 1783, he and his brother Joseph-Michel (also a Freemason) discovered that hot air is lighter than cool air and that this fact could be used to create a way to float above the ground. The first flight had only a few witnesses, while the next one gathered an audience of three hundred thousand. As a result of this achievement, the Montgolfier brothers began a new era in aviation history, which today has its development in space exploration. In doing so, they left a lasting mark on the history of technological progress.

The two Montgolfier brothers were initiated in 1784 into the lodge 'Les Neuf Soeurs' ('The Nine Sisters') in Paris. Benjamin Franklin, the Worshipful Master of this lodge, was one of the witnesses to the second flight of their balloon.

GEORGE WASHINGTON

*Knowledge is, in every country,
the surest basis of public happiness.*

George Washington, First Annual Address, January 8, 1790.

George Washington (1732-1799) was the first president of the United States and one of the most distinguished figures in the history of the country. His main contribution to humanity lies in the role he played as leader of the Continental Army during the War of Independence and as the first president of the United States. Washington was involved in many of the decisive battles and campaigns that led to the end of the war and the independence of the United States. His leadership and determination were crucial to victory. After the war ended, Washington served as President from 1789 to 1797, leading the country during its formation as a new state and the implementation of its Constitution. Washington's presidency was important for establishing and maintaining democratic traditions in the United States, as well as for shaping its position on the international stage. George Washington is called the father of the American nation, and his contribution to the history of the world is difficult to overestimate.

George Washington joined a Masonic lodge in Fredericksburg, Virginia, at the age of twenty in 1752. During the War of Independence, he participated in Masonic ceremonies, also supporting lodges formed in the army. At his first presidential inauguration in 1791, he took the oath of office on a Bible from 'St. John's Lodge' in New York. During his two terms in office, he received Masonic delegations from several states. He presided over the Masonic cornerstone laying ceremony for the US Capitol in 1793 (he took part wearing an apron he received from another prominent Freemason – War of Independence hero – General Lafayette). In retirement, Washington became the Worshipful Master of the newly formed 'Alexandria Lodge № 22.' He was buried with Masonic honors.

ERASMUS DARWIN

Till o'er the wreck, emerging from the storm,
Immortal Nature lifts her changeful form:
Mounts from her funeral pyre on wings of flame,
And soars and shines, another and the same.

Erasmus Darwin

Erasmus Darwin (1731-1802) was an English philosopher, poet, and physician who made significant contributions to the development of natural science. He was the author of a poetic work on evolution, "The Temple of Nature," in which he predicted the existence of DNA. This book was the inspiration for the creation by his grandson, Charles, of the epoch-making work "On the Origin of Species."

He was initiated at the age of twenty-three at 'St. David's Lodge № 36' in Edinburgh in 1754. After moving to Derby, England, in 1788, he joined 'Canongate Kilwinning Lodge № 2' in Scotland. Details of his lodge activities are unknown, but his membership in Freemasonry continued in his family – his son Francis Darwin and grandson Reginald Darwin also belonged to a lodge.

HORATIO NELSON

My character and good name are in my own keeping.
Life with disgrace is dreadful.
A glorious death is to be envied.

Horatio Nelson's letter to his wife

Admiral Horatio Nelson was one of the most important military men of his time. He took part in many naval battles, showing remarkable ingenuity, intuition, and initiative (as well as insubordination) that led to spectacular victories. The greatest of these he achieved was at the Battle of Trafalgar in 1805, in which he defeated Napoleon Bonaparte's French fleet. This battle, which Nelson won, although he died in the process, ensured the British fleet's undivided domination of the seas and enabled the expansion of Britain's naval empire for the next hundred years. Nelson is considered one of Britain's greatest national heroes, and his achievements and position in naval and military history are undeniable.

Nelson most likely belonged to the 'Friendship № 100' lodge in Yarmouth. On the back of a stone commemorating the establishment of this lodge is an inscription in honor of Nelson as a Freemason. His affiliation is confirmed by the Freemasons' Quarterly Review of 1839.

PRINCE HALL

Be always ready to give an answer to those that ask you a question;
give the right hand of affection and fellowship to whom it justly belongs;
let their color and complexion be what it will; let their nation be what it may,
for they are your brethren, and it is your indispensable duty to do so.

Prince Hall

Prince Hall (1748-1807) was an influential abolitionist and a pioneer in issues of equality and civil
rights for African Americans in the United States.
Among other things, he supported the fight to
abolish slavery and obtain equal voting rights and
lobbied for educational rights for African American
children. He was also active in the Back-to-Africa
movement. Hall tried to win a place for New York's
enslaved and free blacks in Freemasonry, education,
and the military, which were among the most crucial
spheres of society in his time. His contribution to the
history of the movement for rights and equality for
African Americans is invaluable, and he can be
considered one of the most influential African American leaders in US history.

Hall is considered the founder of "black Freemasonry" in the United States, known today
as Prince Hall Freemasonry. He formed the African Grand Lodge of North America, was
unanimously elected its Grand Master, and was active in it until his death in 1807.
Thanks to his efforts, African American Freemasons were able to gain recognition and
equality on a par with white Freemasons.

JOSEPH HAYDN

Young people can learn from my example that something can come from nothing. What I have become is the result of my hard efforts.

Joseph Haydn

Franz Joseph Haydn was one of the most important and influential classical composers, counted along with Mozart and Beethoven among the so-called three Viennese classics. Haydn's unique contribution to the history of the world is the development and elaboration of musical forms that became the foundations of classical music. His works are characterized by harmonious structure, subtle rhythm, and melodiousness. Nevertheless, his works from 1760-1770, created in the "storm and stress" (Sturm und Drang) style, using original chords and rare minor keys, although created within the framework of classicism, laid the foundation for the emergence of the Romantic style in music.

Haydn was initiated in 1785 at the lodge 'Zur Wahren Eintracht' ('Under the True Consent') in Vienna. He was encouraged to join by Mozart.

JOHANN GOTTLIEB FICHTE

*The majority of men could sooner be brought to believe themselves
a piece of lava in the moon than to take themselves for a self.*

Johann Gottlieb Fichte

Johann Gottlieb Fichte (1762-1814) was one of
the most important philosophers of the German
Enlightenment. His main contribution to world
history was the development of the philosophy of
German idealism, which was an important part
of European culture in the 19th century. Along
with Friedrich Schelling and Georg Hegel, he is
counted among the trinity of great philosophers
of German classical idealism. In opposition to
Kant, Fichte rejected the possibility of a reality
independent of the cognitive subject (the so-called
thing-in-itself), believing that consciousness is a
fundamental component of reality. His theories
introduced a new approach to philosophical issues
such as cognition, morality, and spirituality and
were an important contribution to the development
of political and social thought.

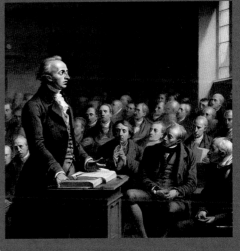

In 1793 Fichte was admitted to the Danzig lodge 'Eugenia zum gekrónten Lówen'
('Eugenia under the crowned lion'). He also belonged to the 'Pythagoras of the Flaming
Star' workshop in Berlin. He was a very committed Freemason, developing his own
interpretation of the philosophy of Freemasonry, believing, among other things, that
Freemasonry should actively contribute to promoting progress in the field of just laws
and reform in the state.

JAMES WATT

It is not worth my while to manufacture in three countries only, but I can find it very worthwhile to make it for the whole world.

James Watt

James Watt (1736-1819) was one of the most important engineers and inventors of the late 18th and early 19th centuries, making significant contributions to industry and technology. Born in Scotland, Watt began his career as an engineer but soon became interested in steam engines. His most important invention was an improvement to the steam engine that allowed more efficient and effective use of energy (his machine used four times less fuel than the model used up to that time). This invention became a key element in the Industrial Revolution and was used to power many industries, including textiles and steelmaking. During his life, Watt  registered several patents that show him as a pioneer and one of the most important engineers in history. His contributions to world history are lasting and unforgettable, and his name is still associated with the industrial revolution and technological development.

Watt became a member of the 'Royal Arch' lodge in Glasgow around 1763.

EDWARD JENNER

I shall endeavor still further to prosecute this inquiry, an inquiry
I trust not merely speculative but of sufficient moment to inspire
the pleasing hope of it becoming essentially beneficial to mankind.

Edward Jenner

Edward Jenner (1749-1823) is considered a pioneer in the medical field and
the actual creator of the modern vaccination model. In 1796, Jenner demon-
strated that in order to immunize a
person against smallpox (a common
and deadly disease in his time), it would
suffice to vaccinate a much milder form
of it – cowpox, which has a mild course
and is not fatal, instead of smallpox.
This discovery was a milestone in the
history of medicine because it paved the
way for the use of vaccination on a
widespread scale, thanks to which, in
the course of the lives of subsequent
generations, many dangerous diseases
were defeated (the World Health Orga-
nization in 1980 officially declared smallpox eradicated on Earth). Jenner's contribution to
the history of the world is enormous, as he helped prevent and control the spread of many
infectious diseases, thereby increasing the overall health and life expectancy of people.

Edward Jenner became a Freemason on December 30, 1802, at the 'Lodge of Faith and
Friendship № 449', in Berkeley, England. Ten years later, he became the Worshipful
Master of his lodge.

TSAR ALEXANDER I

Napoleon or I: from now on, we cannot reign together!

(Tsar Alexander I, when Napoleon was losing the Russian campaign of 1812.)

Tsar Alexander I (1777-1825) made history by defeating Napoleon I Bonaparte's Grand Army of approximately 450,000 men, which attacked Russia. The weaker Russian army adopted effective tactics of retreating, destroying everything behind it, and attacking supply transports and scattered enemy troops. Moscow was also burned, the capture of which, in this situation, gave Napoleon nothing. The harsh Russian winter completed the destruction of the French army, which lost more than 95% of its men as a result of this campaign. The Czar ended the war in Paris and was henceforth regarded as the "liberator of Europe." Roughly until 1815, the Czar promoted limited liberalism in his country. However, he later changed his approach. "Freedom," he maintained, "should be limited within just limits. And the limits of freedom are the principles of order."

Alexander I, with characteristic inconsistency, first banned the existence of secret societies in Russia in 1801, then lifted the ban and became a Freemason himself in 1803. In 1821, in the face of growing national liberation impulses in Freemasonry, he issued further orders, this time banning the Craft and forcing lodge members to sign a declaration that they would never again join Masonic associations at home or abroad.

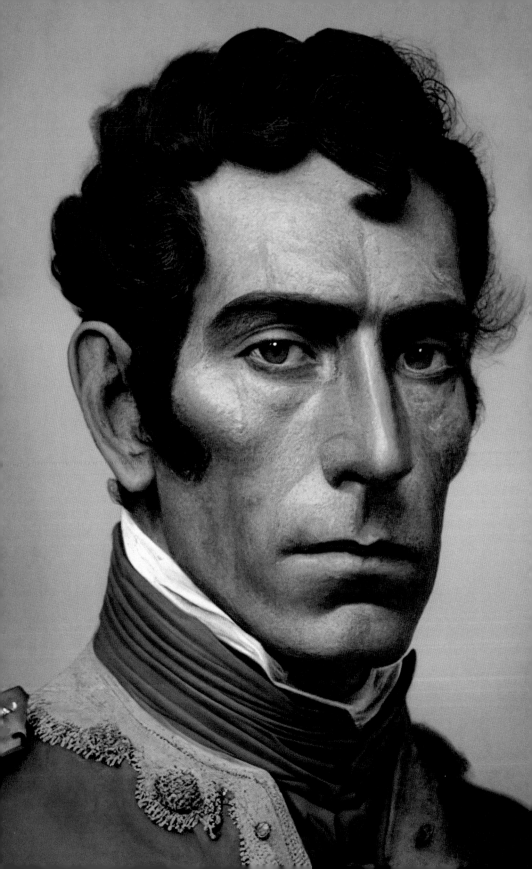

SIMON BOLIVAR

The freedom of the New World is the hope of the Universe.

Simon Bolivar

Simon Bolivar (1783-1830) was one of the main leaders of the revolution in South America, contributing to the independence of Venezuela, Colombia, Ecuador, and eventually Peru and Bolivia. His contribution to the history of the world is that he waged a series of victorious wars and helped create independent states that had previously been Spanish colonies. His activities and struggle for the independence and sovereignty of South American peoples introduced a new pattern for independence movements and was an inspiration to other countries that sought freedom. Bolivar opposed slavery as fundamentally incompatible with the values of a republic based on the principles of freedom and equality.

He was admitted to a lodge in Cadiz, Spain, and later obtained Scottish degrees in Paris, and remained an active Freemason also during his diplomatic mission in London. He was the founder and Worshipful Master of the 'Protectora de las Vertudes № 1' lodge in Venezuela, and in 1824 founded the 'Order and Liberty' lodge in Peru. In 1822 he received the 33rd degree of the Ancient and Accepted Scottish Rite. His Scottish Rite apron and collar can be seen in the museum of the Grand Lodge of New York.

JAMES MONROE

The best form of government is that which is most likely to prevent the greatest sum of evil.

James Monroe

James Monroe (1758-1831), the fifth president of the United States, made a significant contribution to world history through his involvement in foreign policy and the shaping of American diplomacy. He is remembered as the author of the so-called Monroe Doctrine, which was published in 1823 and formed one of the cornerstones of American foreign policy in the 19th century. The doctrine stated that the United States would not tolerate any European intervention in Latin America, which meant that it would defend the independence of countries in that part of the world (and its interests at the same time). In this way, Monroe set the direction of US foreign policy, which had a significant impact on the subsequent fate of the American continent.

James Monroe was admitted to Freemasonry at 'Williamsburg Lodge № 6' in Virginia on November 9, 1775. His continued Masonic activity is confirmed by the minutes of 'Cumberland Lodge № 8' in Tennessee dated July 8, 1819.

SIR WALTER SCOTT

The race of mankind would perish did they cease to aid each other.
We cannot exist without mutual help.
All, therefore, that need aid have a right to ask it from their fellowmen,
and no one who has the power of granting can refuse it without guilt.

Sir Walter Scott

Sir Walter Scott (1781-1832) was one of the most prominent Scottish writers of the 19th century. He is considered the creator of the historical novel genre, which combined fact and fiction and depicted the life of different eras. Scott influenced the fate of the world not only as a writer but also as a promoter of Scottish culture and history. His works encouraged people to visit Scotland and learn about its beauty and traditions. Scott also inspired many other authors and artists who drew on his style and subject matter. Scott's novels were translated into many languages and were extremely popular with readers. Some of his most famous works are "Ivanhoe," "Rob Roy," "Waverley" and "The Bride of Lammermoor." Sir Walter Scott remains an important figure in the history of world literature.

In March 1801, he was admitted to the 'Lodge of St. David' in Edinburgh, where he subsequently attained the degrees of Fellowcraft and Master Mason.

GOETHE

Everybody wants to be somebody; nobody wants to grow.

Johann Wolfgang von Goethe

Johann Wolfgang von Goethe (1749-1832), playwright, novelist, scholar, and politician – is considered the most prominent representative of German literature. In Weimar, he met Charles Augustus, the heir to the throne, with whom he befriended and became his advisor. Since 1792, at his request, Goethe was engaged in the creation of the theater, which he directed until 1817, while actively working on the development of all cultural and educational institutions in the state, leaving his lasting mark in many cultural fields. His greatest works – "The Sufferings of Young Werther" (1774), "Erlking" (1782),

and "Faust" (1808) – have entered the canon of great literature, and Goethean physics (the most famous example of which is the color theory – Farbenlehre) to this day provides an alternative to the materialist Newtonian paradigm.

Goethe was initiated at the 'Amelia' lodge in Weimar in June 1780, received the degree of Fellowcraft on June 23, 1781, and was elevated to Master Mason on March 3, 1782.

PEDRO I

I swore to the Constitution, but even if I didn't swear to it,
it would be a second religion for me.

Pedro I

Pedro I was the founder and first ruler of the Empire of Brazil. He was born in Lisbon as the son of King John VI. In 1807 he fled with his parents to Brazil before Napoleon's invasion of Portugal. In 1821, he was appointed regent of Brazil by his father, who had returned to Europe. A year later, he declared Brazil's independence and assumed the title of emperor. Pedro I was a proponent of constitutionalism and freedom. He adopted Brazil's first Constitution in 1824 and granted voting rights to all free men. He later fought Portugal for recognition of Brazilian independence and defeated it in 1825. In 1831, he abdicated in favor of his son Pedro II and returned to Portugal, where he became king as Pedro IV. There he fought a battle with his brother Miguel, who wanted to restore absolutism. Pedro IV strengthened the Portuguese Constitution and secured the succession of his daughter Maria II. He died of tuberculosis in Lisbon in 1834. Pedro I was an important figure in Brazilian and Portuguese history and a national hero of both countries.

Pedro I was a Freemason. After the country's independence, he appointed his advisor and lodge brother José Bonifácio as the first Grand Master of the Grand Orient of Brazil.

ALEXANDER PUSHKIN

Moral maxims are surprisingly useful on occasions
when we can invent little else to justify our actions.

Alexander Pushkin, Tales of Belkin

Alexander Pushkin (1799-1837) was one of the most important Russian poets and writers and is considered the father of Russian literature. He is considered the most outstanding representative of Russian Romanticism, next to Mikhail Lermontov. His poetry is characterized by vivid language, expressive style, and strong emotions, and the works he created contain strong political and social messages. Pushkin was also a pioneer in the field of poetic novels, in which he combined elements of poetry and prose. His best-known work, "Eugene Onegin," is considered a classic of Russian literature and is still read and studied around the world. Pushkin was also an influential political and social activist, and the views he held on justice and equality are clearly drawn in his works. He was a reformer of the Russian literary language, his works have inspired many subsequent generations of artists and intellectuals, and the influence he has had on Russian culture and literature is inestimable.

Pushkin was initiated in 1821 at the 'Ovid' lodge in Chisinau.

BERNARDO O'HIGGINS

*Aristocracy is naturally abhorrent to me,
and adored equality is my idol.*

Bernardo O'Higgins

Bernardo O'Higgins (1778-1842) was a South American revolutionary and the first leader of Chile. From his teenage years, he was convinced that all South American countries should gain sovereignty. His position in the independence movement was influenced by the fact that his father was the viceroy of Peru. O'Higgins, in alliance with Jose de San Martín, led an armed uprising against Spain, defeating its troops at Chacabuco in 1817. The following year he proclaimed the independence of the Republic of Chile, becoming its dictator. He took care of education, infrastructure development, and the expansion of the army (including the navy). Not  fluent in the intricacies of politics, conflicting with the clergy, the conservative oligarchy, and part of the army, he was forced by the opposition to step down in 1823; he died in exile in Peru.

O'Higgins participated in the late 1790s in London in the work of the influential 'Great American Reunion Lodge' founded by Venezuelan revolutionary Francisco de Miranda. It brought together many Brothers who were close to the cause of Latin American independence.

Well, may the boldest fear and the wisest tremble when incurring responsibilities on which may depend our country's peace and prosperity and, in some degree, the hopes and happiness of the whole human family.

James Knox Polk

James Knox Polk was the 11th President of the United States, serving in office from 1845 to 1849. His main contribution to world history lies primarily in the expansion of the territory of the United States during his time as President. Polk was determined to make his country a world power. Accordingly, he acquired large tracts of land belonging to Mexico, making it possible to expand the borders of the United States from the Nueces River to the Pacific Ocean. Polk, therefore, led the creation of the state of California, which greatly strengthened the country's economy and military position. Polk also gained the state of Oregon for the US as a result of successful  negotiations with Great Britain. In addition, his reign was a time of intense reform and modernization. Overall, the presidency of James Knox Polk was an important period in US history and secured his place in the annals of history as one of the most significant presidents in the country's history.

Polk was admitted to Freemasonry in 1820, served as Junior Warden, and earned the Royal Arch degree. In 1847, he participated in the Masonic ritual of laying the cornerstone of the Smithsonian Institute in Washington.

SAN MARTIN

You will be what you must be, or else you will be nothing

José de San Martín

José de San Martín (1778-1850) was born in Yapeyú, in present-day Argentina. At the age of seven, he left with his parents for Spain, where he began his military career. He fought against France and England in Europe and Africa. In 1812, he returned to South America to join the revolution against Spain. He organized the Andean army and led it across the mountains to Chile. There he defeated the Spanish governor in two decisive battles (in 1817, he and Bernard O'Higgins won a victory over the Spanish army at the Battle of Chacabuco) and secured Chile's independence. He then moved north to Peru,  declaring that country's independence in 1821. Recognizing the importance of Simón Bolívar in the mission to liberate the continent, he made way for him, handing him the role of commander-in-chief of the liberation army. San Martín left South America and settled in France, where he spent the rest of his life. He died there in 1850 of pneumonia. José de San Martín remains a symbol of freedom and democracy for three nations: Argentina, Chile, and Peru.

The liberator of Argentina, Chile, and Peru was initiated at the 'Integridad de Cadiz' lodge, in the Spanish city of Cadiz, in 1808. After some time, San Martin became affiliated with 'Caballeros Nacionales Lodge № 3' (also in Cadiz), where he received the rank of Master Mason on May 6, 1808. After a brief stay in Seville, he lived in London for four months, where he participated in the founding of 'Caballeros Racionales Lodge № 7' ('Rational Gentlemen's Lodge № 7'). On May 24, 1814, San Martin founded the 'Lautaro de Cordoba' lodge. He remained an active Freemason. His mortal remains rest in a mausoleum inside the Buenos Aires Metropolitan Cathedral. However, because San Martín was a Freemason, the mausoleum was placed in the outer wing of the cathedral.

LORD WELLINGTON

I am but a man.

Lord Wellington

Lord Wellington (1769-1852) – born Arthur Wesley (later Wellesley) in Dublin, Wellington was educated in France, did his military service in Flanders, was posted to India in 1796, and returned with a knighthood in 1805. After two years as a Conservative member of parliament in Ireland, he returned to active service, contributing to the victory of Britain's triple alliance with Spain and Portugal against France on the Iberian Peninsula in 1814. Wellington's greatest achievement was defeating Napoleon at Waterloo on June 18, 1815. This victory opened his doors wide to the world of politics, and on January 9, 1828, he was appointed prime minister. One of  his achievements was to get the Catholic Emancipation Act (which allowed Catholics to sit as MPs and take public office) passed in 1829.

Wellington was initiated on December 7, 1790, at 'Trim Lodge № 494' in Ireland. This is the lodge where his father and brother were already Masters. However, except for the day of his own initiation, he never attended another Masonic meeting and was struck from the membership list in 1795.

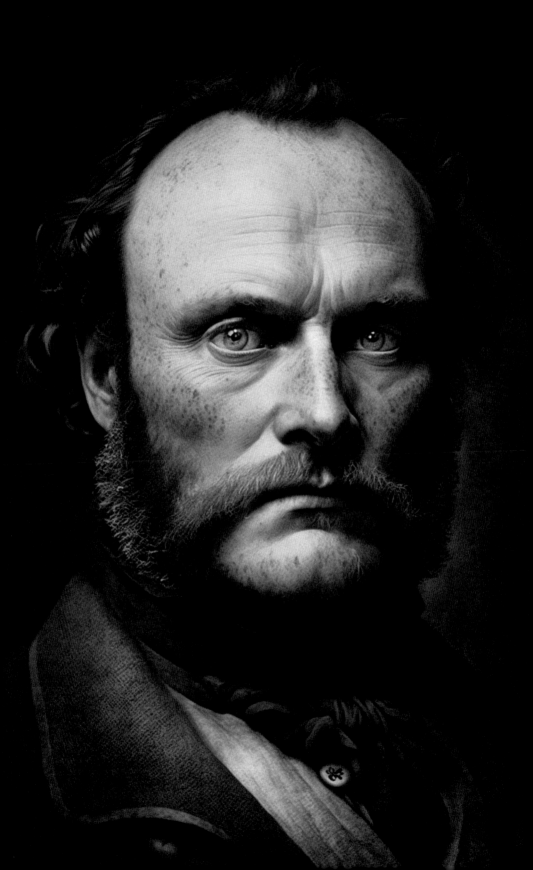

SAMUEL COLT

God created all men, but Samuel Colt made them equal.

(A saying commonly known in the Wild West)

Samuel Colt (1814-1862) was an American inventor, entrepreneur, and designer who made significant contributions to the history of firearms. At the age of twenty-one, in 1835, he invented and introduced the world's first mass-produced, six-shot revolver. This weapon was significant in both the military and civilian spheres, providing users with greater firing speed and efficiency. Colt's invention contributed to the development of modern mass production. His company, Colt's Manufacturing Company, became one of the most important gun manufacturers in history and still exists today.

Samuel Colt was a Freemason, as was his rival Daniel Leacitt, who patented the first revolver model after the Colt, and Richard Gatling – the inventor of the machine gun. Colt had been a member of 'St. John's Lodge № 4' in Hartford, Connecticut, since 1851.

PIERRE-JOSEPH PROUDHON

I do not wish to be either ruler or ruled.

Pierre Joseph Proudhon

Pierre Joseph Proudhon (1809-1865) was born in Besançon, France. He was the son of a poor brewer and self-taught. He worked as a printer, journalist, and writer. In his works, he criticized capitalism, the state, and religion and preached libertarian and egalitarian ideas. He considered himself an anarchist and a mutualist (mutualism is a system based on voluntary cooperation among people without the intermediation of the state or the market). Proudhon opposed private property as a form of theft and inequality. He argued that true property is the ownership of what one has produced or used through labor or need. In 1848, he took part in the revolution against the July monarchy and entered parliament as a representative of the working people. There he demanded social reforms and decentralization of power in favor of the federation of rural and urban communes. His views influenced later anarchist thinkers such as Bakunin (a Freemason as well) and Kropotkin. He died in 1865 in France from lung disease.

Proudhon became a Freemason on January 8, 1847, at the 'Sincérité, Parfaite Union et Constante Amitié' lodge in Besançon.

GIUSEPPE MAZZINI

So long as you are ready to die for humanity,
the life of your country is immortal.

Giuseppe Mazzini

Giuseppe Mazzini (1805-1872) was an Italian lawyer, journalist, and activist for the unification of Italy (Risorgimento). His greatest contribution to world history was the creation of the concept of a "Europe of nations," or the idea of freedom and democracy for all the peoples of Europe. Mazzini was also the founder and leader of revolutionary organizations such as Young Italy, Young Europe, and Young America. The goal of these organizations was to overthrow the monarchy and create republics based on national and social principles. Mazzini took part in many uprisings against Austrian and French rule in Italy. He was also one of the  main inspirers of Garibaldi's Thousand Red Shirts expedition in 1860, which led to the unification of southern Italy with the Kingdom of Sardinia. Mazzini wrote many works on political, religious, and philosophical subjects, such as "On the Duties of Man," "God and Humanity," and "On European Democracy." Being a steadfast republican, he did not recognize the Kingdom of Italy.

Giuseppe Mazzini has been named the Past Grand Master of the Grand Orient of Italy.

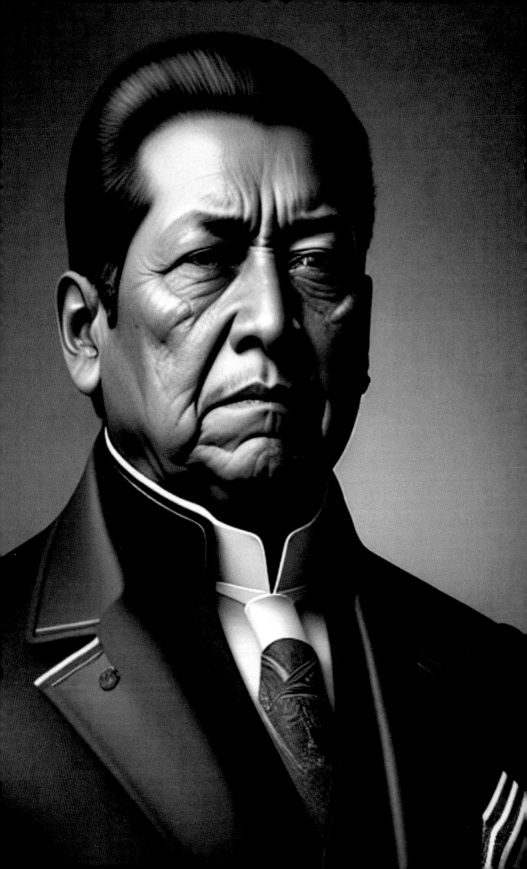

BENITO JUAREZ

Respect for the rights of others means peace

Benito Juarez

Benito Juarez (1806-1872) was a Mexican president and one of the most prominent figures
in the history of his country. His main contribution to world history was his role as a reformer and modernizer of Mexico. Juarez began
his career as a lawyer and attorney and took
office as President in 1858. The period of his
rule is known as the "Great Reform" (La
Reforma). There was a liquidation of church
property, the army was placed under civilian
control, and a number of important social,
legal, and fiscal reforms were carried out. His
most important work was the enactment of the
federalist Constitution of Mexico in 1857,
which established freedom and equality for all citizens regardless of race or origin. In his
actions, Juarez always insisted on respect for the law and civil liberties, was a consistent
democrat, an advocate of equal rights for Native Americans, the reduction of the church's
influence, and a defender of Mexico's sovereignty. All this made him one of the most
significant leaders of his time. To this day, he is considered a symbol of the struggle for
freedom and equality in Mexico and throughout Latin America.

Historians of Freemasonry agree that Benito Juarez was a Freemason, but they do not
have a common opinion on the degrees he held. It seems most likely, however, that he
has received at least the 18th degree of the Memphis rite (the Rose Croix degree).

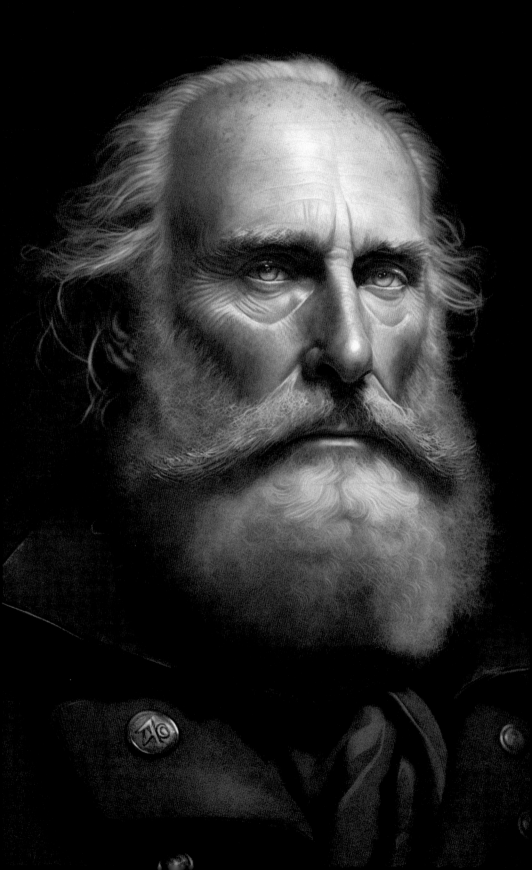

GIUSEPPE GARIBALDI

The day the peasants will be educated in the truth,
tyrants, and slaves will be impossible on Earth.

Giuseppe Garibaldi

Giuseppe Garibaldi (1807-1882) was an Italian revolutionary, soldier and politician, democrat and republican who played a key role in the unification of Italy under the Savoy dynasty. In 1833, he joined the secret organization Young Italy, which had as its goal the unification of Italy. He was a leader of the Red Shirts, a group of volunteers who fought against Bourbon forces in Sicily and Naples. In 1860, he commanded the expedition of a Thousand to Sicily – a thousand red-shirted volunteers under his com-mand overthrew Bourbon rule in the Kingdom of the Two Sicilies, which became a great inspiration for Italians to continue the struggle. His victories contributed to the creation of the Kingdom of Italy in 1861. He later took part in Italy's Third War of Independence against Austria in 1866, capturing the city of Trento. Garibaldi was also active in other countries and supported republican and national liberation movements in South America and Europe, such as supporting the French Communards movement during the siege of Paris in 1870 and commanding the Army of Alsace-Lorraine against Prussia. Garibaldi is considered one of the greatest commanders of modernity and one of Italy's "fathers of the fatherland."

At the age of 26, in 1833, he became affiliated with the Italian Carbonarii, a paramasonic secret revolutionary organization against absolutism and the papacy, working for Italian unification and democracy. In Masonic lodges, he received significant support in organizing the expedition of a Thousand to Sicily. Following its success, he was elevated to the rank of Master Mason in 1860. In 1864, Italian Freemasons elected him Grand Master (he held the office for a year), and in 1865 the Constituent Assembly meeting in Genoa granted him the title of "First Mason of Italy, Honorary Grand Master." From 1866 he was also Honorary Grand Master of the Supreme Council of Sicilian Freemasonry. In 1881, Garibaldi merged the Memphis and Misraim rites and became the Grand Hierophant of the Memphis-Misraim rite.

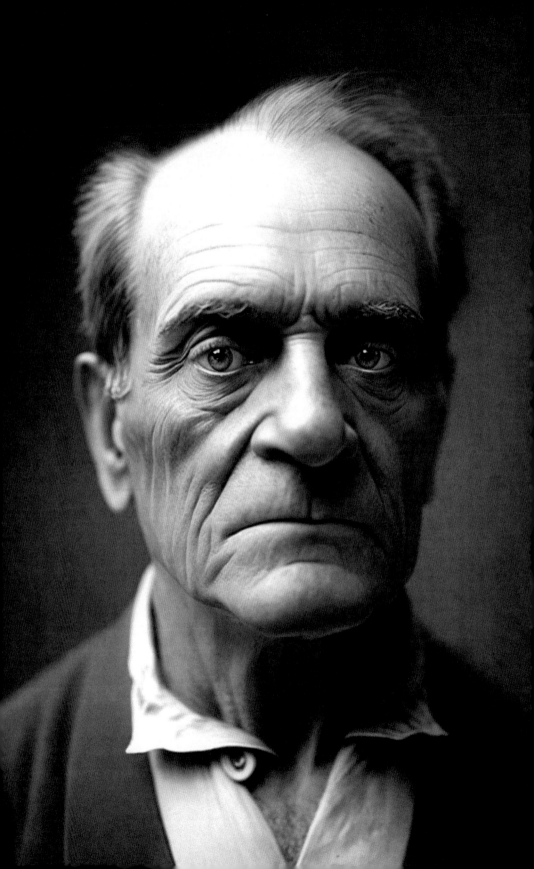

LOUIS BLANC

From each according to his ability, to each according to his need.

Louis Blanc

Louis Blanc (1811-1882) was a French socialist politician and historian. As a young man, he became involved in the creation of "cooperative workshops" (ateliers sociaux), a kind of combination of a labor union and a cooperative. Within such workshops, workers of different professions were to unite their efforts for the common good. Over time, Blanc became one of the leaders of the Radical and Socialist Movement, introducing many social and political reforms. His most important work was the publication of "Organization of Labor" ("Organisation du Travail"), in which he described his vision of socialism. In this concept, Blanc proposed the creation  of state-owned workplaces where everyone would be guaranteed decent and stable employment. His ideas and speeches helped inspire other socialists and leftist movements in France and Europe. Blanc was also an active participant in the Spring of Nations in 1848, and his political and social activities contributed to the development of the concept of socialism.

He belonged to the Order of Memphis and was a member of its Supreme Council of the 33rd degree. He was also an active participant in the meetings of the lodge 'La Grande Loge des Philadelphes.'

LEON GAMBETTA

Despotism and freedom of the press cannot exist together.

Leon Gambetta

Léon Gambetta (1838-1882) was a French lawyer and republican politician who proclaimed the French Third Republic in 1870 and played a significant role in its initial government. He was one of the leaders of the opposition against Emperor Napoleon III and his foreign policy. After France's defeat in the Franco-Prussian War on September 4, 1870, he proclaimed the establishment of the Republic at Paris City Hall. He became Minister of the Interior and organized the country's defense against Prussia. Opposed to surrender to the Prussians, he escaped from besieged Paris by balloon, formed a government of national  defense in Tours, and raised another army. He tried to continue fighting in the provinces but had to sign an armistice after the fall of Paris. He advocated peace on honorable terms and opposed the surrender of Alsace-Lorraine. He was one of the main supporters of maintaining the republic after the fall of the empire. He worked with Adolphe Thiers, the first president of the Third Republic, and introduced educational, military, and administrative reforms. He was the parliamentary majority leader and prime minister of France from November 1881 to January 1882. Gambetta was involved in the formation of French democracy, including the creation and implementation of the Third Republic's Constitution. His influence on the development of democracy in France and Europe is lasting and significant.

Initiated in a Masonic lodge in Bordeaux. On July 8, 1875, he was affiliated with the 'La Clemente Amitie' lodge in Paris.

FRANZ LISZT

I carry a deep sadness of the heart,
which must now and then break out in sound.

Franz Liszt

Franz Liszt (1811-1886) was a Hungarian composer and pianist prominent in Romanticism. He inherited his interest in music from his father, who played the piano, violin, and guitar and performed at the court of Prince Nikolaus II Esterházy. Liszt introduced many innovations to music, such as new piano techniques, and influenced the development of symphonic poem and rhapsody, which became essential elements of Romantic music. His unique sound and style earned him great international fame during his lifetime. As a leading representative of the Romantic movement, he inspired and still inspires many musicians today. He was also a philosopher, wrote essays and articles, and was active in the political arena. His music is still beloved and widely played today, and his influence on culture and the arts continues.

He was initiated in 1841 at the 'Unity' ('Zur Einigkeit') lodge in Frankfurt am Main. He received his second and third degrees in 1842 in Berlin at the 'Under the Three Globes' lodge.

WILHELM I

It's hard to be emperor under such a chancellor.

Wilhelm I on his relationship with Otto von Bismarck.

Kaiser Wilhelm I (1797-1888) was regent and later king of Prussia of the Hohenzollern dynasty and the first German emperor. He became the co-founder of the Second German Reich, which was established after Prussia's victory in the Franco-Prussian War in 1871. His reign was a period of Germany's economic, cultural, and military growth. Kaiser Wilhelm I was known as the "Prince of the Carters" after his brutal suppression of the Baden uprising in 1848 and as the "white-bearded" emperor after the medieval Emperor Frederick Barbarossa. Wilhelm I was not an independent ruler. His chancellor was Otto von Bismarck, who led Germany's foreign and domestic policy, aiming to unify it under the hegemony of Prussia and maintain the balance of power in Europe. Bismarck was also a conservative and opposed liberal and socialist influence in the German parliament, though he did introduce some social reforms, such as health and pension insurance for workers, to gain their support. Wilhelm I was a proponent of conservatism and enlightened absolutism, a form of government based on strong monarchical power, but seeking to improve the living conditions of his subjects through enlightenment reforms.

Wilhelm I was initiated into Freemasonry at a combined meeting of the Grand Officers of the three Grand Lodges of Prussia on May 22, 1840. He became the protector of the Grand Lodge of Prussia. He is known to have been photographed in military uniform, wearing Masonic regalia.

VICTOR SCHŒLCHER

The republic no longer intends to make distinctions in the human family.
It excludes no one from its immortal motto:
liberty - equality - fraternity.

Victor Schœlcher

Victor Schœlcher (1804-1893) was a French abolitionist activist who made a significant contribution
to world history through his efforts to abolish
slavery. He began advocating for slaves and
fighting for their freedom as early as the age of 20.
He was involved in numerous campaigns and
protests and participated in the Haitian uprising
that led to the end of slavery in Haiti. In 1848, as
a member of the French government, Schœlcher
pushed through the enactment of a decree that
ended slavery in France and its colonies. His work
and determination helped free hundreds of thousands of slaves and began the process of banning

slavery around the world. Victor Schœlcher remains one of the most significant abolitionist
activists in history, and his contribution to the struggle for freedom and equality is invaluable.

Schœlcher belonged to the Paris lodge 'Les Amis de la Vérité,' part of the Grand Orient
of France.

JULES FRANCOIS SIMON

*Education is the process by which one mind forms
another mind, and one heart, another heart.*

Jules Francois Simon

Jules Francois Simon (1814-1896) was a philosopher, politician, and educator, one of the most
important French theorists in the field of education.
He served as French Minister of Education (1871-
1873) and later as Prime Minister (1876-1877).
In his writings and speeches, Simon delineated an
innovative concept of education that emphasized
the individual path of development and self-reliance.
His concepts put into practice, against which
clerical circles protested, significantly chan-ged the
educational environment in France and around the
world. In the political field, Simon was a supporter
of democracy and civil liberties, which resulted in
his support of many political reforms in France.

Jules Francois SImon was initiated on July 3, 1870, at the 'Masonic Awakening' lodge
('Le Réveil maçonnique') in Boulogne-sur-Seine.

OSCAR WILDE

Selfishness is not living as one wishes to live;
it is asking others to live as one wishes to live.

Oscar Wilde

Oscar Wilde (1854-1900) was an Irish writer, playwright, and poet who made significant contributions to cultural history. His
satirical and ironic approach to life and
society set new directions in literature. His
most famous works, such as "The Portrait
of Dorian Grey," "Salome," and "The Importance of Being Earnest," have become literary classics and continue to be staged and
read around the world. Wilde was a controversial figure, as he was one of the first
publicly homosexual artists to experience
ostracism from society, trial, and imprison-
ment (the court sentenced him to two years

of hard labor for his homosexuality, which destroyed his health, and he died in poverty
shortly after leaving prison). His life and work influenced the movements for LGBTQ+ rights
and civil liberties, and his writings are considered important to cultural history.

Wilde was initiated in 1875 at the 'Apollo Lodge' in Oxford.

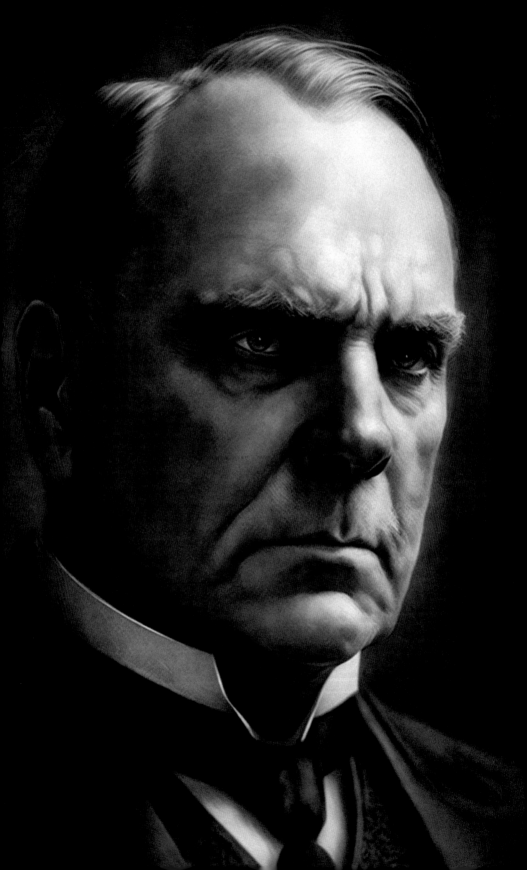

WILLIAM MCKINLEY

The free man cannot be long an ignorant man.

William McKinley

William McKinley (1843-1901) was the 25th President of the United States, and his main contribution to world history was his efforts to develop and expand US territory. McKinley led a war with Spain that soon led to its relinquishment to the US of Cuba, the Philippines, Puerto Rico, and Guam. He was also involved in developing the US economy, introducing protectionist policies that aided the country's industrial development. Shortly after he was elected to a second term, he was shot during a meeting with voters by an assassin who believed McKinley was guilty of widespread social injustice. A few days after the assassination attempt,  the President died. McKinley's contributions to the development of the country and the expansion of its territory were important to the process of the United States becoming a world power.

William McKinley was an active Freemason. He received the first three degrees of initiation in the 'Hiram № 21' lodge in Winchester, Virginia. He also belonged to the system of higher degrees of the York Rite and other Masonic bodies (such as the Knights of Pythias).

SWAMI VIVEKANANDA

*We are what our thoughts have made us,
so take care about what you think.*

Swami Vivekananda

Swami Vivekananda (1863-1902) was one of India's most influential philosophers and spiritual masters of the 19th century, contributing significantly to the promotion and development of Hinduism and yogic philosophy throughout the world. As a young man, Vivekananda studied philosophy, religion, and literature and followed the teachings of his mentor, Ramakrishna, who taught that every religion is a doorway to the same God. In 1893, Vivekananda addressed the Chicago Religious Conference, where he presented Hinduism as a universal religion that offers a path to spiritual development for all people, regardless of race, nationality, and background. His talk resonated, and Vivekananda became a well-known and respected speaker and spiritual teacher, giving lectures and courses in Europe and the United States from then on. Upon his return to India, he founded the Ramakrishna Mission, which became known as one of the most important charitable and spiritual organizations in the country, working for spiritual development, education, and environmental protection. His teachings and philosophy on freedom, justice, and equality for all people, as well as his contributions to the development and promotion of Hinduism, make him an important and influential figure in the history of the world.

Swami Vivekananda was initiated on February 19, 1884, became Fellowcraft on March 15, 1884, and was elevated to the degree of Master Mason on May 20, 1884, at 'Anchor and Hope Lodge № 1'.

FREDERIC A. BARTHOLDI

*I would hope to glorify freedom and liberty over there [America]
in the hope that it may be regained over here [France.]*

Frederic Auguste Bartholdi on the Statue of Liberty

Frederic Auguste Bartholdi (1834-1904) was a French sculptor whose contributions to world history
include his most famous sculpture, the "Statue of
Liberty" (its full name is "Liberty Illuminating the
World"), which became one of the symbols of the
United States. Bartholdi was inspired by the
design of the Suez Canal and planned to build a
huge lighthouse at one of its entrances, resembling
the Colossus of Rhodes, and although this design
never came to fruition, years later, it was reflected
in the Statue of Liberty, given to the United States
by France to mark the centennial of the Declaration
of Independence. Work on the Statue lasted from
1876 to 1882, with Gustave Eiffel, the designer of
the Eiffel Tower, assisting the artist in designing

its skeleton. Bartholdi also introduced new sculptural techniques, such as the use of sheet
metal and iron, to make the sculptures lighter and more durable. His contributions to the
history of art and architecture are widely recognized and place him on the list of the most
important sculptors in history.

In 1875, Bartholdi was initiated into the 'Alsace-Lorraine' Lodge in Paris.

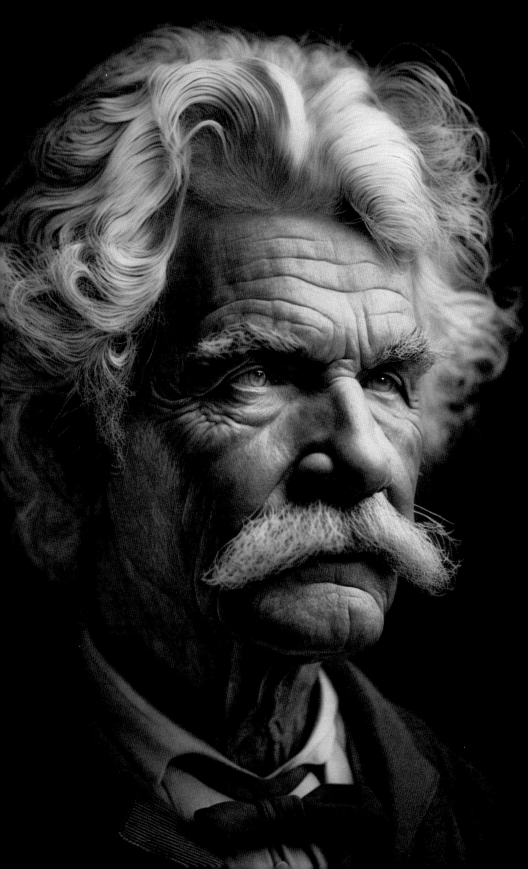

MARK TWAIN

Whenever you find yourself on the side of the majority,
it is time to pause and reflect.

Mark Twain

Mark Twain (Samuel Langhorne Clemens) (1835-1910) was one of the most important American writers of the 19th century and a committed activist for equality and social justice. He became primarily famous as the author of the novels "The Adventures of Tom Sawyer" and "The Adventures of Huck Finn," which describe the adventurous lives of these boys in the southern states of the United States in the period before the Civil War. Twain was highly critical of slavery and racial discrimination, and his novels showed the brutal realities of black life at the time. He often used humor, irony, and sarcasm in his work to show the absurdity of racism and social injustice.
Twain was one of the first members of the American Association for Racial Equality, which worked to improve the living conditions of African Americans and combat discrimination. Later in life, he continued his social and political activities, supporting various organizations and campaigns for equality and social justice, including serving as editor-in-chief of The Buffalo Express newspaper. Twain's contribution to the struggle for the rights of African Americans was one of the many aspects of his legacy as a writer and social activist. His main contribution to the history of the world was his unique literature, which was critical, humorous, and sensitive to social irregularities. Mark Twain is considered one of the greatest American writers of all time.

On February 18, 1861, Mark Twain was initiated into 'Polar Star Lodge № 79', where he later received the other two degrees of Blue Freemasonry. He was an active Freemason, visiting many lodges in the US and around the world. He made various references to Freemasonry in his books, such as using the term "Great Architect of the Universe" when he wrote about God.

EDWARD VII

No, I shall not give in. I shall go on. I shall work to the end.

Edward VII

Edward VII (1841-1910) was King of the United Kingdom and Emperor of India from January 22, 1901, until his death. His reign brought some relaxation of customs, which were very conservative during the reign of Edward's mother, Queen Victoria. Unlike Victoria, Edward tended not to rule the country directly, focusing instead on performing representative functions. He did, however, make significant contributions to world history, mainly through his diplomatic activities. His reign was a time of relative peace and stability in Britain, as well as an intensification of its international relations, especially with France. Through his  visits to Paris, largely due to his engaging manner, he laid the groundwork for the British-French agreement (although France and Britain had treated each other with distrust and even hostility since Napoleon I) and contributed to the formation of the Triple Alliance (Entente), which included Russia, an alliance that was revived during both the First and Second World Wars. Edward VII was known as the "Peacemaker" and "Uncle of Europe."

Being under the spell of the mysticism and idealism of Freemasonry, he was initiated in Sweden in 1868, then quickly introduced to the higher degrees of the Swedish Rite, and when he returned to England was an active and dedicated Freemason, attending lodge meetings and founding many new ones. Even as King Edward VII of England, he simultaneously served as Grand Master of the United Grand Lodge of England (UGLE).

Jean Henri Dunant (1828-1910) became involved in charity work at an early age, founding a group that helped the poor and visited prisons, as well as establishing a YMCA in his hometown. While working for several organizations, he began traveling abroad. On the evening of June 24, 1859, Dunant arrived in Solferino just as a battle was beginning near the city. Witnessing it and seeing tens of thousands of dying and wounded people left without help, Dunant, deeply moved, decided to take matters into his own hands. He quickly organized a neutral relief effort among the locals, purchased the necessary supplies, and organized temporary hospitals. Upon his return to Geneva, he began to promote his ideas, and after gaining support, he founded the International Committee of the Red Cross in 1863 and initiated talks with the Swiss parliament that led to the signing of the first Geneva Convention. In 1901, Dunant received the Nobel Peace Prize for his work.

Jean Henri Dunant was a member of 'St. David's Lodge № 36'.

EDWARD ABRAMOWSKI

*Egoism is inoculated to people throughout life, starting from childhood,
inoculated by upbringing and by social conditions, by competition,
by the hard struggle for bread, by the reign of money,
by the whole system of slavery.
It is a huge breeding and school of egoism,
in which everyone is educated...*

Edward Abramowski

Edward Abramowski (1868-1918) was a Polish philosopher, psychologist, and social activist. He was born into a wealthy landowning family in what is now Ukraine. He studied philosophy and psychology at universities in Warsaw, Geneva, and Paris. He was one of the pioneers of Polish experimental psychology and sociology and was also concerned with the political and social problems of his era. He was a proponent of anarchism, cooperativism, and participatory democracy. He promoted the idea of grassroots self-organization of society and the concept of a "cooperative republic." Like Leo Tolstoy, Abramowski believed that the revolution would achieve nothing if there was no

moral transformation of the people beforehand. At the same time, he argued that the transformation of the social system should occur quite peacefully, gradually, through the establishment of cooperatives and associations based on mutual aid. His works are still relevant and inspiring to many civic movements.

Between 1908 and 1910, Abramowski spent time in Brussels and Paris, where he joined the order Le Droit Humain and later belonged to the Warsaw lodge of the Grand Orient of France.

THEODORE ROOSEVELT

Do what you can, with what you have, where you are.

Theodore Roosevelt

Theodore Roosevelt (1858-1919) was the 26th President of the United States, and his contributions to the world were significant and multidirectional. Leader of the famous "Rough Riders" in the Spanish-American War, governor of New York, prominent conservationist who championed the creation of the National Park System, Nobel Peace Prize winner, adventurer, who was always looking for new challenges, and, of course, President of the United States. His tenure lasted from 1901 to 1909 and was known as the "Reform Era." Roosevelt was a proponent of developing the American economy and was known as the "Voice of the People" due to his  support for social movements such as the labor rights and environmental movements. During his presidency, institutions such as the US Forest Service and the US Food and Drug Administration were established. Thanks to Roosevelt, medicine developed rapidly in the United States; Americans finally received effective health care. It is also worth appreciating his war policy and the running of the country during the First World War. It is worth mentioning that he is one of three US presidents to receive the Nobel Peace Prize. It was awarded to Roosevelt for his involvement in bringing the war between Japan and Russia to an end in 1905.

Theodore Roosevelt became a Freemason at the age of 42 in 1901, the same year he became President of the United States. As President, he visited Masonic lodges around the country and the world. In 1906, he attended a Masonic ceremony to lay the corner-stone of the House of Representatives building.

ERNEST SHACKLETON

Optimism is true moral courage.

Sir Ernest Henry Shackleton

Sir Ernest Henry Shackleton (1874-1922) was a British polar explorer who led one of the most heroic polar expeditions to Antarctica, with the goal of crossing the ice continent from the Weddell Sea coast to the Ross Sea coast for the first time in history. This mission, known as the Transantarctic Expedition of the Imperial Transantarctic Research Fund, began in 1914 and ended in 1917. Although it did not reach its goal, it is considered one of the greatest achievements of British polar explorers. Shackleton was known for his extraordinary fortitude and leadership skills, which allowed him to survive many dangers during the

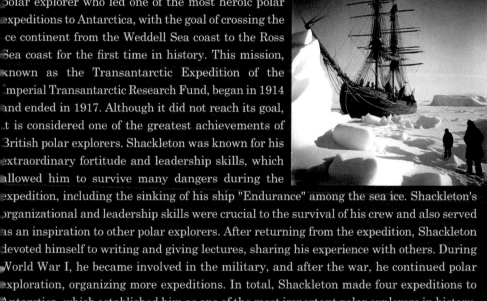

expedition, including the sinking of his ship "Endurance" among the sea ice. Shackleton's organizational and leadership skills were crucial to the survival of his crew and also served as an inspiration to other polar explorers. After returning from the expedition, Shackleton devoted himself to writing and giving lectures, sharing his experience with others. During World War I, he became involved in the military, and after the war, he continued polar exploration, organizing more expeditions. In total, Shackleton made four expeditions to Antarctica, which established him as one of the most important polar explorers in history. His attitude and contributions to the development of polar exploration continue to inspire generations of explorers and travelers.

In 1911, Shackleton was initiated into the 'Guild of Freemen Lodge № 3525' belonging to the United Grand Lodge of England. In the same year, he received his second degree, and on May 30, 1913, he was elevated to the rank of Master Mason.

HARRY HOUDINI

No prison can hold me;
no hand or leg irons or steel locks can shackle me.
No ropes or chains can keep me from my freedom.
My Brain is the key that sets me free.

Harry Houdini

Harry Houdini (1874-1926) was a famous American illusionist and "escape" artist who made significant contributions to the development of the art of magic and entertainment around the world. Houdini is widely regarded as one of the greatest magic artists in history, and the contributions he made to the art of illusion are invaluable. His amazing tricks, such as getting out of handcuffs, locked boxes, and sometimes being placed underwater, always delighted audiences. One of Houdini's most important achievements was to help raise the prestige of the illusionist profession. Instead of treating the art of magic as entertainment for children, Houdini presented it as an art for adults, requiring a serious approach and skill. Houdini was also one of the first artists to start using the media to promote his image and his art. He was a pioneer in advertising, and his media campaigns, such as "Houdini's Challenges," attracted the attention of fans and skeptics alike.

Harry Houdini was initiated at 'St. Cecile Lodge' in New York City in 1923 and advanced to the second and third degrees on July 31 and August 21, 1924. He was proud to be a Freemason and even organized a performance for the Scottish Rite Valley in New York. The event was attended by 4,000 people at the Scottish Rite Cathedral and, in the process, raised a lot of money for Masons in need. Houdini became a Shriner a few weeks before his tragic death in October 1926.

JUAN GRIS

I prefer the emotion that corrects the rule.

Juan Gris

Juan Gris (1887-1927) was one of the most important representatives of Cubism, an avant-garde art
movement that revolutionized European painting
and sculpture in the 20th century. He was born in
1887 in Madrid, where he studied engineering at
the Madrid School of Arts and Sciences. In 1906 he
moved to Paris and ended up at the Bateau-Lavoir,
the artists' house where his compatriot Pablo
Picasso lived. There he began to paint pictures in
the Cubist style, characterized by geometric forms
and a rich color palette. His works marked a new
direction in art, combining the tradition of European painting with the influences of modernism

and modern design. Subjects included mainly portraits and still lifes, which often included
elements of collage. His works depicted a world composed of simple forms and colors, creating
a unique aesthetic and helping to define Cubism as an important trend in art history. Gris
also contributed to the development of Cubist theory through his essays and lectures.
He died prematurely in 1927 of kidney failure.

Juan Gris was initiated into Freemasonry at 'Voltaire' lodge at the same works, during
which the sculptor Jacques Lipchitz was also admitted. Gris, from then on, regularly
and actively participated in lodge meetings.

*I am in favor of helping the prosperity of all countries because,
when we are all prosperous, the trade with each
becomes more valuable to the other.*

William Howard Taft

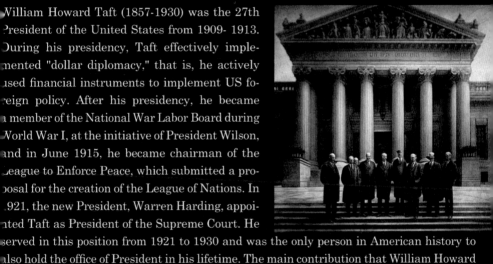

William Howard Taft (1857-1930) was the 27th
President of the United States from 1909- 1913.
During his presidency, Taft effectively imple-
mented "dollar diplomacy," that is, he actively
used financial instruments to implement US foreign policy. After his presidency, he became
a member of the National War Labor Board during
World War I, at the initiative of President Wilson,
and in June 1915, he became chairman of the
League to Enforce Peace, which submitted a pro-
posal for the creation of the League of Nations. In
1921, the new President, Warren Harding, appointed Taft as President of the Supreme Court. He
served in this position from 1921 to 1930 and was the only person in American history to
also hold the office of President in his lifetime. The main contribution that William Howard
Taft made to history lies in his involvement during this period in developing and strengthening
the American legal and constitutional system. His achievements in this field were significant
and lasting and contributed to the consolidation of American democracy.

William Howard Taft became Master Mason at 'Kilwinning № 356' Lodge in Cincinnati,
Ohio, in 1901. Although his many responsibilities did not allow him to be regularly
nvolved in Freemasonry, Taft greatly appreciated and supported the Craft.

There is nothing more deceptive than an obvious fact.

Arthur Conan Doyle, The Tragedy at Boscombe Valley

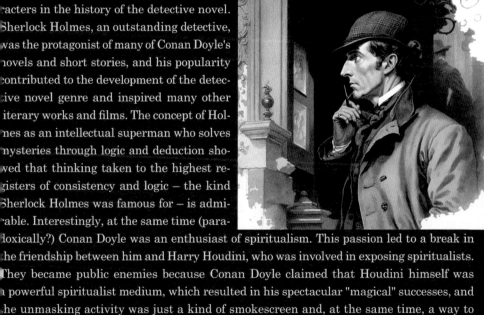

Sir Arthur Conan Doyle (1859-1930) created one of the most famous and influential characters in the history of the detective novel. Sherlock Holmes, an outstanding detective, was the protagonist of many of Conan Doyle's novels and short stories, and his popularity contributed to the development of the detective novel genre and inspired many other literary works and films. The concept of Holmes as an intellectual superman who solves mysteries through logic and deduction showed that thinking taken to the highest registers of consistency and logic – the kind Sherlock Holmes was famous for – is admirable. Interestingly, at the same time (paradoxically?) Conan Doyle was an enthusiast of spiritualism. This passion led to a break in the friendship between him and Harry Houdini, who was involved in exposing spiritualists. They became public enemies because Conan Doyle claimed that Houdini himself was a powerful spiritualist medium, which resulted in his spectacular "magical" successes, and the unmasking activity was just a kind of smokescreen and, at the same time, a way to get rid of the competition.

Conan Doyle was initiated at the age of twenty-seven in 1887 at 'Phoenix Lodge № 257' in Southsea, England. Present at the ceremony was Dr. James Watson, who later became his close friend and model for the famous partner of Sherlock Holmes.

JOSEPH JOFFRE

I don't know who won the Battle of the Marne.
But if it had been lost, I know who would have lost it.

Joseph Joffre, Quote from "The Campaign of the Marne" (1935) by Sewell Tyng

Joseph Joffre (1852-1931) was a French general who commanded the French Army on the Western Front from the beginning of World War I until the end of 1916. He was responsible for developing a plan that called for the concentration of French forces on the German border and an offensive in Alsace-Lorraine. His plan failed and led to heavy losses on both sides. However, Joffre is credited with stopping the German advance during the Battle of the Marne in September 1914, which turned the tide of World War I and is considered one of the most important battles in history. In December 1916, he was appointed Marshal of France and vice-president of the Higher War Council.

He was initiated in 1875 and was a member of the Paris lodge 'Alsace-Lorraine.'

SIR THOMAS LIPTON

Never despair. Keep pushing on!

Sir Thomas Lipton

Sir Thomas Lipton (1848-1931) was a Scottish entrepreneur who founded the Lipton tea empire and gained fame as a sailor. Lipton, who was born in Glasgow to a family of Irish shopkeepers, emigrated to the United States in 1865. There he worked as a laborer and salesman before returning to Scotland and opening his first grocery store in 1871. He soon developed a chain of shops across the UK and began importing tea from Ceylon. His Lipton brand became popular with low prices and aggressive advertising, including offering promotions and contests to entice customers to buy. Thomas Lipton, achieving great success in the trade, tried to make tea, which was then an expen-

sive and exclusive commodity, into a cheap and common product. His company floated shares and became a limited liability company, Lipton Ltd, in 1895, the same year receiving the title of official Royal Court Supplier from Queen Victoria. In 1898 Lipton received a knighthood from the Queen for his charitable work.

Thomas Lipton belonged to the lodge 'Scotia №178' in Glasgow, where he was raised to the degree of Master Mason in 1870. In the year of his death, 1931, he was its oldest member.

JOHN PHILIP SOUSA

To the average mind, popular music would mean compositions vulgarly conceived and commonplace in their treatment. That is absolutely false.

John Philip Sousa

John Philip Sousa (1854-1932) was an American composer and conductor, best known as the composer of military marches. Sousa was born in Washington to a family of Portuguese-German descent. At a young age, he learned to play the violin, flute, clarinet, and guitar and composed his own works. At the age of thirteen, he joined the U.S. Marine Corps orchestra as a student musician and served there for seven years. He later worked as a theater and circus conductor and founded his own civilian orchestra. He also conducted the US Marine Corps orchestra for twelve years (1880-1892). He was called "American March King ."From 1873 until his  death in 1932, he composed 136 marches, many of which have become popular and patriotic symbols of the United States, such as "The Stars and Stripes Forever," "Semper Fidelis," and "The Washington Post."

Initiated in 'Hiram Lodge № 10' on July 15, 1881. In 1886 he attained the degree of Knight Templar, and in 1922 he joined the Shriners, becoming the honorary leader of the Almas Temple Band.

KING CAMP GILETTE

*There is no passion so strong in a man as a desire to learn
when he has reached that plane where he can appreciate
the pleasure derived from the attainment of knowledge.*

King Camp Gillette

King Camp Gillette (1855-1932) was an American
businessman and inventor who designed and
patented a razor with inexpensive thin, disposable
steel blades. His invention revolutionized the
shaving products market and brought him great
financial success. Gillette founded the Gillette
Safety Razor Company in 1901 and sold his razors
all over the world, and his name became syno-
nymous with modern shaving. Gillette co-founded
the socialist movement in the US in the 1890s and
wanted to use the profits from the sale of his safety
razor to finance the implementation of his beliefs
in a new, more just socio-political system. He was

also a social visionary who promoted the idea of a utopian city called Metropolis, where all
humanity would live under one government.

Gillette belonged to 'Adelphi Lodge' in Quincy, Massachusetts, where he was raised to
the rank of Master Mason in 1901. He later belonged to 'Columbian Lodge' in Boston.

ANNIE BESANT

Thought creates character.

Annie Wood Besant

Annie Wood Besant (1847-1933) was a British writer, Theosophist, and activist for women's rights and for Irish and Indian independence. Considered a defender of freedom, she supported both Irish and Indian self-government. She was also a prominent educator and author of more than three hundred books and pamphlets. In 1889 she joined the Theosophical Society and, in 1907, became its second leader after Helena Blavatsky. In 1893 she traveled to India, where she became involved in the national liberation movement. She was one of the first women elected to the Indian National Congress. She was also known as an advocate of birth control and social reform in Britain.

Annie Besant introduced Le Droit Humain Co-Masonry to England with the consecration of the 'Human Duty № 6' lodge in London on September 26, 1902. Crowned with the 33rd degree of the Ancient and Accepted Scottish Rite, she became Grand Commander of the Order of Le Droit Humain.

ANDRE CITROEN

Do not waste your life meditating on your furuncles.

André Citroën

André Citroën was a French entrepreneur and engineer best known as the creator of Europe's first mass-production system for automobiles. In 1919, he founded a car manufacturing company that quickly became one of the leading producers in Europe. He introduced many innovations, such as mass production using an assembly line, as well as groundbreaking car models, such as the Citroen C1 and Type A. In addition, Citroën was a pioneer in product marketing and advertising. He introduced many innovative advertising campaigns, including the first television commercials, as well as car rentals, which allowed customers to test 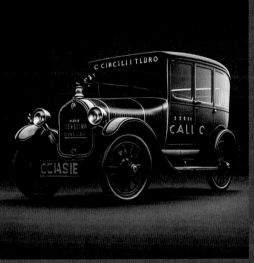 drive cars before buying them. Citroën made important contributions to the automotive industry and became one of the pioneers in marketing and advertising.

Citroën was initiated in 1904 and was a member of the 'La Philosophie Positive' lodge, working in Paris. The origin of the Citroën logo is the subject of controversy. Officially, it has no connection to Freemasonry, but Freemason Philippe Benhamou, a member of the Grand Lodge of France since 1990, has published a text about the possible Masonic origin of the logo. Here is what he says: "it's a well-known and recognized fact: the Citroën brand logo is an interpretation of the compass and the square, two universal symbols of Free-masonry, in 1907. André Citroën was inspired by this symbol when he designed the emblem of his gear factory (a square inscribed in a circle), which a few years later and after several modifications became the company's well-known logo.

RUDYARD KIPLING

I always prefer to believe the best of everybody;
it saves so much trouble.

Rudyard Kipling

Rudyard Kipling (1865-1936) was an English writer
and poet who was born in British India and inspired by
it in his work. He became the author of world-famous
works such as "The Jungle Book," "Kim," and "Just So
Stories." His works, usually set in the British colonies,
reflected his fascination with exotic cultures. He was also
a patriot and promoter of British imperialism, which he
expressed, among other things, in his poems about
British soldiers. In 1907, he won the Nobel Prize for
literature, being the first English-language writer to
accomplish this. His influence on literature and culture
was enormous and continues to this day.

Rudyard Kipling became a Freemason in India, in 1885, at the age of twenty, thanks to
a dispensation granted by the Grand Master. Almost immediately, he became secretary
of his mother lodge, 'Hope and Perseverance № 782'. Already at the age of twenty-four,
leaving India, he ceased to be an active member of his lodge but never severed his
connection with the Craft. In the following years, he visited lodges in other countries.

KEMAL ATATÜRK

Those who use religion for their own benefit are detestable.
We are against such a situation and will not allow it.
Those who use religion in such a manner have fooled our people;
it is against just such people that we have fought
and will continue to fight.

Mustafa Kemal Atatürk

Kemal Atatürk (1881-1938) was a Turkish politician and military officer who created the independent Republic of Turkey after the defeat of the Ottoman Empire in World War I. During the war, he was one of the top commanders of the Ottoman Army and won a victory at the Battle of Gallipoli. After the war, he spearheaded the national movement that resisted the Allies and the Greeks in Turkey's war of independence and resisted the danger of subjecting Turkey to partition. He was Turkey's first president, from 1923 until his death in 1938, and introduced reforms that quickly secularized and modernized the country. He  carried out many social reforms, such as abolishing the caliphate, introducing the Latin alphabet, establishing equal rights for women, and promoting the development of education and culture. He is considered the father of modern Turkey and a national hero.

Kemal Atatürk was initiated in 1907 at the 'Macedonia Risorta' lodge of the Grand Orient of France.

ALFONS MUCHA

Art exists only to communicate a spiritual message.

Alfons Mucha

Alfons Mucha (1860-1939) was a Czech painter and printmaker, best known for his deco-
rative theater posters, characteristic of the
Art Nouveau period, especially those featu-
ring actress Sarah Bernhardt. His trade-
marks are prints depicting idealized female
figures in belle époque style, surrounded by
flowers, leaves, symbols, and arabesques. He
also created illustrations, advertisements,
postcards, and covers. His style combined fin
de siècle, Byzantine, Slavic, and Oriental
elements with modern forms and colors. He
was also a patriot and promoter of Slavic
culture. His greatest work was a series of
twenty paintings on historical and mytholo-
gical themes entitled Slavic Epic. In it, he depicted the fate of the Slavs from ancient times
to the 20th century. He was arrested by the Gestapo after Germany occupied Czechoslovakia
and died shortly after his release. His influence on art and culture was enormous and
continues to this day.

Mucha became a Freemason in Paris in 1898 and, upon his return to Prague, helped
establish the first Czech-speaking lodge there (named after Komensky). In 1923 he was
elected Grand Master of the newly established Grand Lodge of Czechoslovakia. In 1924
he published (under the initials A.M.) a book on Freemasonry, and in 1930 he became
Sovereign Grand Commander of the Supreme Council of the Ancient and Accepted
Scottish Rite in Czechoslovakia. A sizable collection of Mucha's unknown works on
Masonic topics, hidden for 60 years (first from the Nazis, then from the Communist
authorities), was recently discovered. The collection includes symbol-rich paintings,
designs, and sketches of Masonic regalia.

JANUSZ KORCZAK

Look for your own way. Know yourself before you want your children to know you.
Realize what you yourself are capable of before you want to
carve out a range of rights and responsibilities for your children.
Of all, you yourself are the child you must know, raise, and educate above all.

Janusz Korczak

Janusz Korczak, actually Henryk Goldszmit (1878/1879-1942), was a Polish-Jewish physician, educator, writer, and social activist. He went down in history as a pioneer in the struggle for children's rights and the creator of a modern system of raising children in the spirit of respect, self-reliance, and democracy. Janusz Korczak was the director of orphanages for Jewish and Polish children in Warsaw. There he introduced many innovative solutions, such as the children's self-government, the college court, and the orphanage newspaper. He was also the author of many books for children and adults on pedagogical and social issues. Janusz Korczak died in 1942 in the Treblinka death camp. He refused to leave his pupils at the Jewish orphanage and voluntarily went with them to the Warsaw Ghetto and then to the transport to Treblinka. His attitude was an expression of steadfast fidelity to the ideals of humanism and love for children.

Korczak belonged to Freemasonry. He was initiated, at the latest in 1925, into the Polish 'Star of the Sea' lodge of the International Order Le Droit Humain. He was a regular participant in away meetings of Polish Freemasons and theosophists at the Manor House in Mężenin.

HENRI LA FONTAINE

International institutions ought to be, as the national ones in democratic countries, established by the peoples and for the peoples.

Henri La Fontaine

Henri La Fontaine (1854-1943) was a Belgian lawyer, bibliographer, and politician. He served as a professor of international law and was a senator in the Belgian Parliament for 36 years, as well as President of the International Peace Bureau. In 1923, he was awarded the Nobel Peace Prize. Henri La Fontaine was an ardent supporter of internationalism and pacifism. He supported the idea of creating a World Federal Union and a World Court of Justice. He was also involved in the movement for women's rights, popular education, and freedom of conscience. Henri La Fontaine was also an outstanding bibliographer and founder of the Universal Documentary Library

in Brussels. There he collected more than 9 million index cards with information on books, periodicals, and articles in various fields of knowledge. His goal was to create a universal information system for mankind.

La Fontaine was initiated in 1882 at the socially and politically engaged lodge 'Les Amis Philanthropes (n° 1)' in Brussels (the Grand Orient of Belgium). He was the Worshipful Master of this lodge from 1908 to 1911 and from 1922 to 1925. In Freemasonry, as in other fields to which he devoted his energies, he was promoting peace, democracy, and the emancipation of women. Between 1912 and 1928, he helped establish the national federation of the Co-Masonry Order Le Droit Humain in Belgium. In 1913, La Fontaine also helped found the Universal League of Freemasons (ULF), an autonomous body that brings together individual Freemasons regardless of most of the "regularity" rules that divided their lodges. Within the League, Henri La Fontaine organized a pacifist group that sought to win the support of Freemasons at pacifist congresses. He headed the Belgian section, formed in 1929.

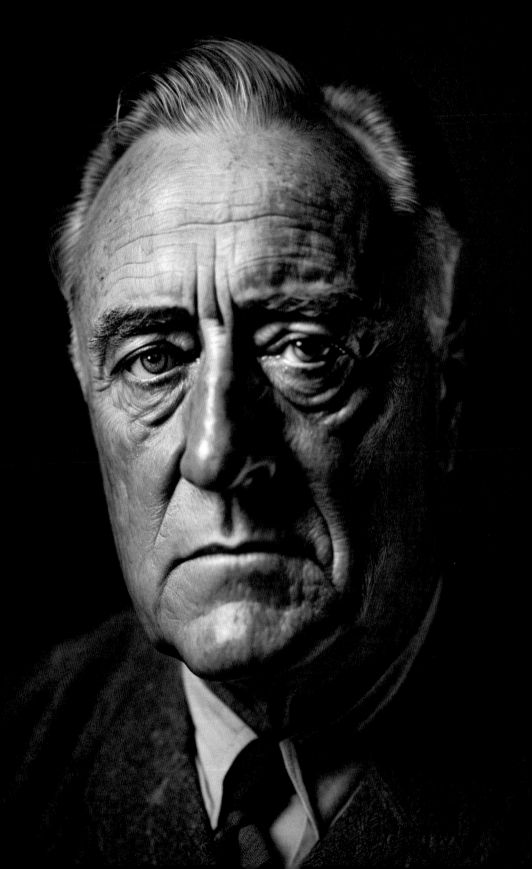

FRANKLIN DELANO ROOSEVELT

The only thing we have to fear is fear itself.

Franklin Delano Roosevelt

Franklin Delano Roosevelt (1882-1945) was an American politician and the 32nd President of the United States. He was the only US president to serve more than two terms in office. He was a member of the Democratic Party and a leader of the New Deal movement. Roosevelt played a key role in dealing with the Great Economic Crisis of the 1930s. He introduced a number of social and economic reforms, such as social security, unemployment benefits, and banking regulation. At the same time, he worked to protect the environment. He made history by leading the United States during World War II in alliance with Great Britain and the Soviet Union. He supported the creation of the United Nations and the Atlantic Charter. He died of a stroke in April 1945, a few weeks before the end of the war in Europe.

Franklin Delano Roosevelt was initiated at 'Holland Lodge № 8' in New York City on October 10, 1911. Eighteen years later, he received the 32nd degree of the Ancient and Accepted Scottish Rite and later joined the Shriners' temple, AAONOMS, in Albany. Roosevelt was also the Honorary Grand Master of the Grand Lodge of Georgia and of the Order of De Molay.

HENRY FORD

There is no failure except failure to serve one's purpose.

Henry Ford

Henry Ford was an American industrialist and founder of the Ford Motor Company, who made significant contributions to world history through the innovations he made in the automotive industry. His greatest achievement was the introduction of the revolutionary concept of mass production of automobiles, which contributed to the development of the automobile industry around the world. Ford introduced many improvements in car manufacturing technology, such as the assembly line and numerous innovations in the assembly system. His introduction of high efficiency and low production costs helped make cars more accessible to a wide audience and changed the way of life in the United States and around the world.

Ford was initiated in 'Palestine Lodge № 357' and was raised to the degree of Master Mason in 1894. He continued his Masonic career throughout his life, which is no mean feat considering his many achievements and successes. In 1940, he received the 33rd and last degree of the Ancient and Accepted Scottish Rite, the culmination of many decades of Masonic service.

JOHN PERSHING

No commander was ever privileged to lead a finer force; no commander ever derived greater inspiration from the performance of his troops.

John Pershing

John Pershing (1860-1948) was an American general who commanded the American Expeditionary Force (AEF) on the Western Front during WWI. His contribution to the history of the world was:
- Ensuring the independence and coordination of American troops in Europe, despite Allied pressure to subordinate them to local command.
- Introducing and developing the potential of new combat tactics and technologies, such as aviation, tanks, and long-range artillery.
- Capturing key German positions at the battles of the Marne, Meuse-Argonne, and Saint-Mihiel.
- Ultimately contributing to the Allied victory over the Central Powers and the end of the war.

In addition, Pershing served as a mentor to many future American generals, such as Dwight Eisenhower, George Patton, and Douglas MacArthur. After the war, he was promoted to General of the Armies of the United States, the highest military rank in US history. He died in 1948 and was buried at Arlington National Cemetery.

He was initiated in 1888 at 'Lincoln Lodge № 79' in Lincoln, Nebraska State.

GEORGE VI

*Together we shall all face the future with stern resolve and prove
that our reserves of willpower and vitality are inexhaustible.*

King George VI

George VI (1895-1952) was King of Great Britain from 1936 to 1952. During his reign, the world experienced major changes, including a world war and political and technological transformation. He was the first king to visit the United States in an attempt to counter isolationist tendencies on the eve of the clash with the Third Reich. George VI was a symbol of the nation's unity during the war, his spirit and courage helping to inspire hope and aid military efforts. He gained the public's respect when he chose not to leave the city during German air raids on London, despite the fact that the royal palace was bombed nine times. During his reign, the British empire crumbled - Ireland, India, Iraq, Jordan, and Burma gained independence, while Palestine was divided into a Jewish and Arab state.

George VI was initiated on December 2, 1919, at 'Navy Lodge № 2612'. He was a Freemasonry enthusiast, belonging to several lodges and various Masonic organizations. He was Grand Master of the Grand Lodge of Scotland (1936), and although he formally withdrew from Masonic activity after becoming king, he personally installed his brother George, Duke of Kent, as Grand Master of the United Grand Lodge of England.

ALEXANDER FLEMING

*It is the lone worker who makes the first advance in a subject;
the details may be worked out by a team, but the prime idea
is due to enterprise, thought, and perception of an individual.*

Alexander Fleming

Alexander Fleming (1881-1955) was a Scottish physician and microbiologist who discovered the first effective antibiotic – penicillin. His discovery was accidental – he noticed that the mold Penicillium notatum grew on one of his bacterial cultures, which inhibited bacterial growth. Fleming published the results of his research in 1929 but failed to isolate pure penicillin or test its effects on humans. It was not until the 1940s that a group of Oxford University scientists led by Howard Florey and Ernst Chain developed a method for producing and testing penicillin on a large scale. Fleming, Florey, and Chain  were jointly awarded the Nobel Prize in Medicine in 1945 for their research on penicillin. The discovery of penicillin was a breakthrough in medical history and in world history. Penicillin saved millions of people from deadly bacterial infections such as pneumonia, tuberculosis, and sepsis. Penicillin also helped reduce the death rate of soldiers during World War II and contributed to the development of new fields of science, such as biotechnology and molecular genetics. Penicillin was the first of many antibiotics that changed the face of medicine and improved the quality of life for people around the world.

At the age of 27, Fleming was initiated into 'Santa Maria Lodge № 2682' in London. In 1942 he became the Worshipful Master of his lodge. He was an active Freemason, also active in other lodges, and in 1934 became Senior Grand Deacon of the United Grand Lodge of England, and in 1948 Past Senior Grand Warden.

JEAN SIBELIUS

Pay no attention to what the critics say.
A statue has never been erected in honor of a critic.

Jean Sibelius

Jean Sibelius (1865-1957) was a Finnish composer and violinist who created music in the style of late Romanticism and early modernism. His music was important to the formation of Finnish national identity and independence. Sibelius drew inspiration from Finnish folklore, mythology, and poetry, especially the epic Kalevala. His best-known works include Finlandia, a symphonic patriotic poem; the Seven Symphonies, full of expression and originality; and the Violin Concerto, the only solo concerto written by Sibelius. Sibelius contributed to world music as one of the most popular composers of the late 19th and early 20th centuries. His music was innovative in form, harmony, and instrumentation. His style evolved from rich melody and color to a more economical and synthetic expression. Sibelius was also an influential teacher and mentor to younger composers. His work was admired by many famous musicians, such as Richard Strauss, Arnold Schönberg, and Igor Strawinski.

Sibelius was initiated in 1922 at the 'Suomi' lodge in Helsinki. As a very active Freemason, he became one of the reactivators of Finnish Freemasonry after it was banned by an edict of Czar Alexander I in 1822.

LOUIS B. MAYER

America must remain, at any cost, the custodian of freedom, human dignity, and economic security.

Louis B. Mayer

Louis B. Mayer (1884-1957) was a Canadian American film producer and co-founder (in 1924) of Metro-Goldwyn-Mayer (MGM). For nearly 30 years, he was the most powerful man in Hollywood, managing the most prestigious film studio that brought together the biggest stars, directors, and screenwriters. Mayer was the creator of the "star system," which involved promoting and controlling actors and actresses by signing long-term contracts with them. Among his discoveries were Greta Garbo, Clark Gable, Judy Garland, and Elizabeth Taylor. Mayer contributed to the development of American cinema as an art and industry. His films were often  based on classic novels or plays, as well as on patriotic and moral themes. Mayer was also politically and socially active. He was one of the founders of the Academy of Motion Picture Arts and Sciences and the originator of the Academy Awards. He was also a philanthropist and supported many charitable and educational organizations.

Mayer was a member of 'St. Cecile Lodge № 568' in New York.

CECIL DE MILLE

The person who makes a success of living is the one
who sees his goal steadily and aims for it unswervingly.

Cecil De Mille

Cecil De Mille (1881-1959) was an American film
producer, director, screenwriter, and actor. He
became one of the pioneers of American cinema
and the creator of many epic historical and
religious films. His movies were characterized by
grandeur, rich sets and costumes, and numerous
mass scenes. De Mille directed more than 70 films
during his 50-year career. Among his best-known
works are "The Ten Commandments" (1923 and
1956), "King of Kings" (1927), "Cleopatra" (1934),
"Samson and Dalila" (1949), and "The Greatest
Show on Earth" (1952). His films won many
awards and nominations, including an Academy
Award for Best Picture for "The Greatest Show on
Earth." De Mille had a major impact on American and world culture. His films often inspired
other filmmakers and introduced new cinematic techniques. De Mille was also socially and
politically active. He was one of the founders of the Hollywood Anti-Nazi League and an FBI
collaborator in the fight against "communism ."He was also a philanthropist and supported
many cultural and educational institutions.

Cecil De Mille was initiated at the 'Prince of Orange № 16' lodge in New York.

ICHIRO HATOYAMA

*Under the banner of liberalism, we will devote ourselves
to a Fraternal Revolution, avoid extreme left-wing and right-wing
ideologies, and work steadfastly to achieve a healthy and vibrant
democratic society and build a free and independent cultural nation.*

Ichirō Hatoyama, 1953

Ichiro Hatoyama (1883-1959) was a Japanese politician who served as Prime Minister of Japan from 1954 to 1956. He was one of the leaders of the conservative camp and opposed the occupation policy of the United States. He looked to normalize relations with the Soviet Union and China and regain Japan's sovereignty. Hatoyama was also a co-founder of the Liberal Democratic Party (PLD), which dominated Japan's political scene for most of the time after World War II. He was the party's first chairman and prime minister. Under his rule, Japan began a process of economic and social reconstruction and introduced educational and administrative reforms.
Hatoyama was also one of the few Christian politicians in Japan. His religious views were influenced by his wife, Kaoru, who was a Baptist. Hatoyama supported Christian missionary and charitable activities in Japan and engaged in interreligious dialogue.

Hatoyama received the degree of Entered Apprentice in 1951, and it was only after he became prime minister that he asked to continue his Masonic journey. Due to the fact that Hatoyama was an invalid, the 2nd and 3rd degrees were granted to him on the same day, March 26, 1955, at the Tokyo Lodge № 125.

GEORGE MARSHALL

The only way human beings can win a war is to prevent it.

George Marshall

George Marshall (1880-1959) was an American general and politician who played a key role in leading the US war effort during World War II and in shaping the post-war international order. He was Chief of Staff of the US Army from 1939 to 1945 and worked with Presidents Franklin Roosevelt and Harry Truman, as well as with Allied leaders such as Winston Churchill and Joseph Stalin. Marshall also served as US Secretary of State from 1947 to 1949 and as US Secretary of Defense from 1950 to 1951. As head of diplomacy, he proposed the so-called Marshall Plan, a program of economic aid for the reconstruction of Europe after the war. The plan helped  stabilize the continent, curb the expansion of communism, and strengthen the transatlantic alliance. Marshall is considered one of the most outstanding American military men and politicians of the 20th century. He received many honors and awards, including the Nobel Peace Prize in 1953 for his contribution to world peace.

Marshall was made a Freemason "at sight" by the Grand Master of the District of Columbia in 1945.

CLARK GABLE

*I'm just a lucky slob from Ohio who happened to be in the right place
at the right time. The only reason they come to see me is that
I know that life is great, and they know I know it.*

Clark Gable

Clark Gable (1901-1960) was an American film actor, often
called the "King of Hollywood." During his 37-year career, he
starred in more than 60 films of various genres. He began his
career by appearing in the theater, later playing modest roles
in silent films from 1924 to 1926. From the early 1930s, his
popularity began to grow, and he began to take on roles of
confident and commanding amateurs. He is best known for
his role as Rhett Butler in Gone with the Wind, which brought
him legendary fame and for which he received an Oscar
nomination. He was also a war hero, serving as a bomber pilot

during World War II from 1942 to 1944. Clark Gable brought his talent, charm, and
courage to the fate of the world. He was an icon of the "Golden Era of Hollywood" and
an inspiration to generations of viewers and actors.

Clark Gable belonged to 'Beverly Hills Lodge, № 528', where he was elevated to the
degree of Master Mason in October 1933.

DOUGLAS MACARTHUR

Only those are fit to live who are not afraid to die.

General Douglas MacArthur

General Douglas MacArthur (1880-1964) was one of the most famous and successful generals of the US Army. He was the commander of the Allied armies in the southwestern theater of operations in the Pacific during World War II. He achieved the rank of General of the Army (equivalent to a marshal) as one of only five American officers (only John Pershing, post-humously George Washington, and Ulysses Grant received the higher military rank). He led the US Army and allies to victory over Japan. When the Korean War broke out, Mac-  Arthur headed the UN intervention force, formed for the first time in history and made up of contingents from 17 countries. He almost won the war, but when 300,000 "volunteers" from China unexpectedly joined in, the intervention force was pushed on the defensive, and eventually, President Truman brought about an armistice. MacArthur, who had strongly urged a declaration of war against China, was dismissed. Toward the end of his life, MacArthur advised President Johnson against intervention in Vietnam, predicting that it would be fought under even more adverse conditions than in Korea. MacArthur was known for his unique military strategy. His remarkable contribution to world history is primarily his role in leading the US Army and allies to victory over Japan in World War II and preventing Communist forces from seizing all of Korea.

While stationed in the Philippines, MacArthur was made a Freemason "at sight" by the Grand Master of the Philippines, an extremely high honor reserved for exceptional cases. On January 14, 1936, he was elevated to the degree of Master Mason, and on March 28 of the same year, he received the 32nd degree of the Ancient and Accepted Scottish Rite. Despite his many responsibilities, MacArthur managed to remain active as a Freemason.

WINSTON CHURCHILL

Never give in.

Winston Churchill

Winston Churchill (1874-1965) was one of the most significant politicians of the 20th century, and his main contribution to world history is the role he played in leading Britain during World War II. Churchill headed the British government in 1940, at a time when the Nazis under Hitler were trying to subjugate Europe. He pushed through a hard line against Germany and fought tenaciously against them until the Allied victory in 1945. After the war, he remained an important player on the international stage, working with other leaders, such as Harry S. Truman, in developing peacetime plans. Winston Churchill was one of the first politicians to support the idea of European unification. He was the initiator of the creation of the "United States of Europe." He is often recognized (e.g., in a 2002 BBC poll) as the most outstanding Briton of all time.

Churchill was initiated into 'Studholme Lodge № 1591' (now 'United Studholme Alliance Lodge') on May 24, 1901. He advanced to the second degree almost two months later, on July 19, and was elevated to Master Mason on March 25, 1902.

NAT KING COLE

If you smile through your fear and sorrow,
Smile, and maybe tomorrow
you'll see the sun come shining through
for you.

Nat King Cole

Nat King Cole (1919-1965) was an American jazz pianist and singer. He was known for such hits as "Unforgettable," "Mona Lisa," and "The Christmas Song." Nat King Cole has contributed his unparalleled voice, style, and class to the history of mankind. He was one of the first African American artists to gain popularity among white audiences and contributed to the fight against racism in the music industry. His work also helped open doors for other African American artists who had difficulty gaining recognition and success in an industry ruled by whites. He was also a forerunner in television show business, hosting his own show, The Nat King Cole Show, from 1956 to 1957, and was inducted into the Rock and Roll Hall of Fame in 2000.

Nat King Cole was a member of 'Thomas Waller Lodge № 49', PHA (Prince Hall Freemasonry) in Los Angeles since 1938. The lodge was formed by African American musicians.

CAMILLE HUYSMANS

The upbringing of youth must be very strict in a free country
because it takes a drill to practice freedom reasonably.

Camille Huysmans

Camille Huysmans (1871-1968) was a Belgian politician and philologist. He served as prime minister of
Belgium from 1946 to 1947. He was also secretary of
the Second Socialist International. He was also a
leader of the movement pushing for greater autonomy
for Flanders within Belgium. As prime minister, he
faced a royal crisis caused by the controversial attitude
of King Leopold III during World War II. Camille
Huysmans was a socialist and social reformer. He
supported the improvement of the living and working
conditions of workers, the development of the edu-
cational and cultural system, and the equality of
women. He was also a friend of the Jewish people and the Zionist movement. He showed
a friendly attitude toward Jewish immigrants in Antwerp between 1920 and 1940 and
supported the establishment of a Jewish state in Palestine. In Israel, there are streets
named after him in the cities of Netanya and Haifa.

Camille Huysmans was a member of the lodge 'Les Amis Philanthropes (n° 1)' in Brussels
(the Grand Orient of Belgium).

JOHN STEINBECK

And this I believe: that the free, exploring mind of the individual human is the most valuable thing in the world.

John Steinbeck

John Steinbeck (1902-1968) was an American writer and journalist. He won the 1962 Nobel Prize in literature for his realistic writing, which combined humor and social sensitivity. He wrote thirty-three books, many of which are considered classics of American literature. His best-known works include "East of Eden," "The Grapes of Wrath," and "Of Mice and Men." In his works, he depicted the lives of simple people during the Great Depression, war, and migration. His style was simple but rich in metaphors and symbols. Steinbeck's influence on literature and culture is enormous. He inspired many writers, such as Ernest Hemingway and Cormac McCarthy. His works are still read and appreciated by modern readers.

John Steinbeck belonged to 'Salinas Lodge № 204' in California, where he was initiated on March 1, 2029, advanced to the second degree on April 12, 1929, and was elevated to the Master Mason degree on May 24, 1929.

HARRY TRUMAN

Actions are the seed of fate deeds grow into destiny.

Harry S. Truman

Harry Truman was the 33rd president of the United States from 1945 to 1953. His presidency was associated with key events in world history, such as the end of World War II, the beginning of the Cold War, and the creation of the United Nations. He made the decision to use atomic weapons against Japan in August 1945, which led to that country's surrender and the end of the Pacific War. He was also one of the main architects of the post-war international order and co-founder of the United Nations. Truman pursued a policy firmly opposed to the expansion of communism and the influence of the Soviet Union. He introduced the "Truman Doctrine," which

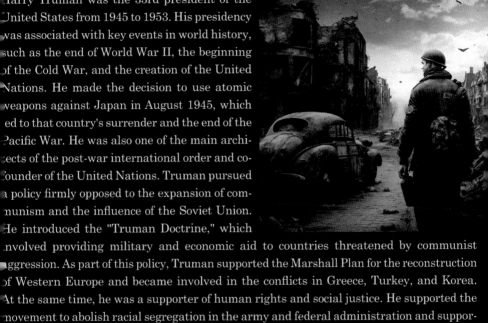

involved providing military and economic aid to countries threatened by communist aggression. As part of this policy, Truman supported the Marshall Plan for the reconstruction of Western Europe and became involved in the conflicts in Greece, Turkey, and Korea. At the same time, he was a supporter of human rights and social justice. He supported the movement to abolish racial segregation in the army and federal administration and supported the introduction of universal health care. He was also the first American President to recognize the state of Israel shortly after its proclamation in 1948. His decisions as the leader of the free world and defender of democracy had long-term consequences for human history.

Truman was a very active Freemason, including during his duties as a senator and later as vice president and President of the United States. He was initiated on February 9, 1909, at 'Lodge № 450' in Belton. From 1912 to 1917, he attained successive degrees in the Ancient and Accepted Scottish Rite and later in the York Rite. From 1940 to 1941, he was the Grand Master of the Grand Lodge of Missouri. In October 1945, he was crowned with the 33rd degree of the Ancient and Accepted Scottish Rite. On May 18, 1959, he was celebrating his 50 years of active service in Freemasonry.

LYNDON B. JOHNSON

Books and ideas are the most effective weapons
against intolerance and ignorance.

Lyndon B. Johnson

Lyndon B. Johnson (1908-1973) was the 36th President of the United States and took office after the
assassination of John F. Kennedy in November
1963. As President, Johnson introduced a series of
social reforms known as the "Great Society," which
aimed to improve the living conditions and education of Americans and combat poverty and racial
discrimination. Johnson signed into law the Civil
Rights Acts of 1964 and 1968, which banned racial
segregation and provided voting equality for African Americans. Johnson was particularly involved
in foreign policy, escalating the Vietnam War, which
caused much controversy and protest at home and
abroad. Also worth mentioning is his support for technological and scientific development,
including space programs. Johnson did not seek re-election in 1968 and died five years later.

Johnson was a member of 'Johnson City Lodge № 561, in Johnson City, Texas. He received only the degree of Entered Apprentice and chose not to continue his Masonic work.

SALVADORE ALLENDE

I am certain that my sacrifice will not be in vain; I am certain that,
at the very least, it will be a moral lesson that will punish
felony, cowardice, and treason.

Salvadore Allende

Salvadore Allende (1908-1973) was Chile's first socialist president. Taking office in 1970, he was the first Marxist to come to power through democratic elections in Latin America. His main contribution to world history is his attempt to create a socialist state in Latin America that was based on the principles of equality and social justice. Allende introduced many social and economic reforms, such as nationalizing key sectors of the economy, increasing wages and pensions, expanding health care and education, and improving the rights of women and indigenous peoples. Allende faced many problems and adversities during his presidency, such as inflation, recession, labor, and agricultural strikes, CIA sabotages, and resistance from the right and the military. In the view of Soviet officials, Allende's fundamental mistake was his unwillingness to use "justified" violence to fight the opposition. Resistance from domestic and foreign conservative forces ultimately led to his overthrow and death in a 1973 coup. Allende remains, especially in Latin America, a symbol of the struggle for social justice.

Allende belonged to the 'Progresso 4' lodge in Valparaíso. It is worth mentioning that he was killed during the right-wing coup by General Pinochet, who was also a Freemason.

DUKE ELLINGTON

Jazz is the only unhampered, unhindered expression of complete freedom yet produced in this country.

Duke Ellington

Duke Ellington, actually Edward Kennedy Ellington (1899-1974), was an American pianist, composer, and leader of his own jazz orchestra from 1923 until his death in 1974. He was one of the greatest and most influential jazz composers in history. Ellington wrote more than two thousand compositions that covered a variety of musical styles and forms. Duke used all possible sources of inspiration in them, from classical music and spirituals to ragtime and blues. Some of his most famous pieces include "Mood Indigo," "Take the A Train," "It Don't Mean a Thing (If It Ain't Got That Swing)," and "Caravan." Ellington collaborated with many prominent jazz musicians, such as Billy Strayhorn, Johnny Hodges, Ben Webster, and Ella Fitzgerald. Ellington also pioneered the creation of long jazz pieces of a symphonic or operatic nature, such as "Black, Brown and Beige," "Such Sweet Thunder," and "Sacred Concerts." Ellington has received many awards and honors for his contributions to American and world culture, including the Presidential Medal of Freedom and the Pulitzer Prize. His works are considered timeless and continue to introduce new generations to the world of jazz.

He belonged to 'Social Lodge #1' (Prince Hall Freemasonry) in Washington

VANNEVAR BUSH

To pursue science is not to disparage the things of the spirit.
In fact, to pursue science rightly is to furnish
the framework on which the spirit may rise.

Vannevar Bush

Vannevar Bush (1890-1974) was an American engineer, inventor, and scientific administrator who, during World War II, headed the Office of Scientific Research and Development (OSRD), through which almost all military development research was conducted, including important advances in radar and the atomic bomb. He was also the creator of the Differential Analyzer, one of the first analog computers. After the war, Bush wrote the famous report "Science – The Endless Frontier," in which he proposed the creation of the National Science Foundation (NSF) as a government agency to support basic scientific research. Bush is also considered a prophet of digital technology thanks to his 1945 essay "As We May Think," in which he introduced the concept of hypertext and a device called the memex, which was to be a personal archive of information for each user. Vannevar Bush is considered one of the most significant and influential engineers and scientists in the history of American science and technology.

Vannevar Bush was an active Freemason, serving as Worshipful Master at 'Richard C. Maclaurin Lodge' in Cambridge, Massachusetts.

CHARLES LINDBERGH

After my death, the molecules of my being will return to the Earth and the sky. They came from the stars. I am of the stars.

Charles Lindbergh

Charles Lindbergh (1902-1974) was an American aviator who gained international fame in 1927 after he became the first man to fly solo and uninterrupted across the Atlantic Ocean in his Spirit of St. Louis aircraft. Lindbergh was also a military man, author, inventor, and activist. He collaborated with Robert Goddard in experiments on rocket development and with Alexis Carrel in research on organ perfusion. Lindbergh was also involved in political and social issues. He opposed US participation in World War II and supported isolationism and the America First movement. After the war, Lindbergh became an advocate of environmental and wildlife protection and promoted better relations between the US and the USSR.

Lindbergh received the rank of Master Mason in 1926 at 'Keystone Lodge № 243' in Missouri - just months before his historic flight brought him worldwide fame. Although little is known about his Masonic accomplishments, Lindbergh wore a pin with the square and compasses during his flight, and The Spirit of St. Louis was adorned with the Masonic emblem. As the Scottish Rite Journal wrote,

As a hero of aviation, Lindbergh stood for all that the public thought of as essentially American: Independence, self-reliance, courage, and perseverance. At a time when the West had been won and most thought the frontier gone, Lindbergh showed there was another kind of frontier to explore through science and technology. Lindbergh, as a Freemason represents a long line of explorers and adventurers down through the ages who were members of the Craft. From Lewis and Clark to polar explorers to astronauts such as E. "Buzz" Aldrin who walked the surface of the moon – testament to the spirit of Freemasonry, all!

JOSEPHINE BAKER

Surely the day will come when color means nothing more than the skin tone,
when religion is seen uniquely as a way to speak one's soul,
when birth places have the weight of a throw of the dice,
and all men are born free when understanding breeds love and brotherhood.

Josephine Baker

Josephine Baker (1906-1975) was a French dancer, actress, singer, and intelligence agent of African American descent. Her career flourished mainly in Europe, especially in France, where she became a symbol of jazz and African culture. Her dancing and performances were considered unique and original. As one of the first African American women to gain popularity and international recognition, Baker was also active in the struggle for human rights and racial equality. During World War II, she worked with the French Resistance and provided intelligence to the Allies. After the war, she became involved in the civil rights  movement in the United States and performed at many demonstrations and charity concerts. Baker was also known for her humanitarian work and her adoption of 12 children from different countries and cultures, which she called her "rainbow family." Josephine Baker remains a symbol of commitment to equality and justice.

Josephine Baker was initiated on March 6, 1960, in one of the lodges of the Grande Loge Féminine de France (Grand French Lodge of Women).

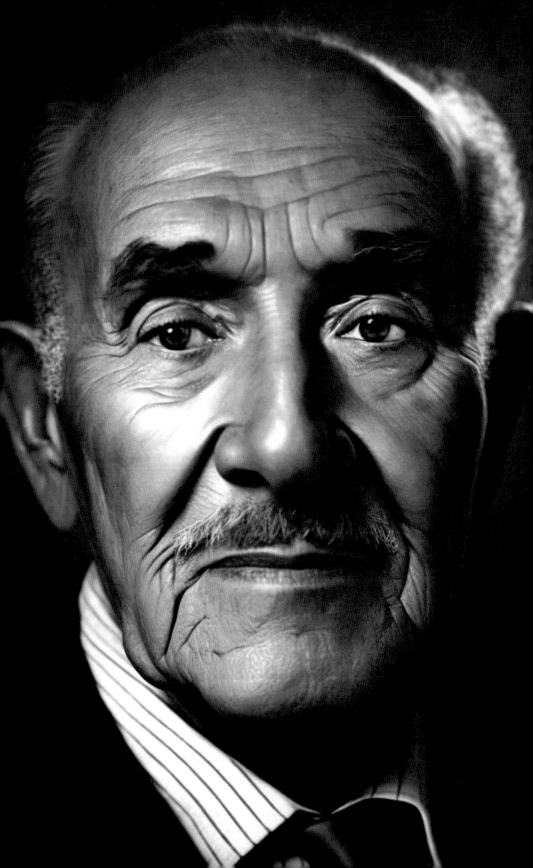

JACK WARNER

It's funny how the harder I work, the most successful I become.

Jack Warner

Jack Warner (1892-1978) was a Canadian American film producer and entrepreneur who was one of the founders, President, and driving force behind Warner Bros. studio in Burbank, California, which became one of the largest and most innovative film studios in cinema history. His career spanned some 45 years and exceeded that of any other of Hollywood's pioneering film magnates. He created and promoted many famous and influential films, such as "Casablanca," "Yankee Doodle Dandy," and "My Fair Lady." He was also one of the first producers to introduce sound into films using the Vitaphone system. Warner was also a founding member of the Ame-

rican Academy of Motion Picture Arts and Sciences, which awards the Oscars and was also involved in charity and politics. His contribution to world history was to develop and set standards in the film industry, which contributed to the development and popularity of cinema as an entertainment and form of art.

Warner was a member of 'Mount Olive Lodge № 506' in California.

JOHN WAYNE

I want to play a real man in all my films, and I define manhood simply:
men should be tough, fair, and courageous, never petty,
never looking for a fight, but never backing down from one either.

John Wayne

John Wayne (1907-1979) was an American actor, director, and film producer who became an iconic figure through his roles in westerns and war films. He was one of Hollywood's greatest legends and a symbol of American individualism and patriotism. In his time, he became the quintessential American, as a noble, chivalrous, heroic cowboy. He starred in more than 140 films, making the values of the Wild West famous around the world in films such as "Stagecoach," "The Searchers" and "Rio Bravo." Wayne received an Academy Award for Best Actor in a Leading Role in "True Grit" and many other awards and honors. The  American Film Institute ranked him 13th on its list of the greatest actors of all time. He was at the same time an active, and over time – even after his death – increasingly controversial defender of conservative political and social values.

John Wayne belonged to 'Marion McDaniel Lodge № 56' in Tuscon, Arizona. He practiced both the higher degrees of the York Rite as well as the Ancient and Accepted Scottish Rite (he was granted the 32nd degree of the Rite). He also belonged to the Shriners.

HARLAND DAVID SANDERS

*I'm against retiring. The thing that keeps
a man alive is having something to do.*

Colonel Sanders

Harland David Sanders (1890-1980) was an
American entrepreneur and founder of the
KFC (Kentucky Fried Chicken) brand, which
is one of the world's largest and best-known
chains of fast-food restaurants. His portrait is
used as the logo of this company. In 1965, after
many years of experimenting, Sanders brought
into the history of gastronomy his recipe for
chicken fried in 11 herbs and spices. People
loved the taste, and Sanders established the
first KFC restaurants, which quickly became
popular and began to expand globally. In doing
so, he introduced a new business model and
style of eating that is now widespread around

the world. Sanders was also an active philanthropist and supported many charitable and
educational organizations. He received the title of honorary colonel of the state of Kentucky
and many other awards and honors. All in all, Sanders made a significant contribution to
world history as a pioneer of the fast-food industry.

Sanders earned his first three degrees at 'Lodge № 651' in Henryville, Indiana, in 1919
and later affiliated with 'Hugh Harris Lodge № 938' in Corbin, Kentucky, in 1953.

COUNT BASIE

*The real innovators did their innovating
by just being themselves.*

Count Basie

Count Basie (1904-1984) was an American jazz
pianist, composer, and bandleader. He was one
of the most important and influential jazz
musicians of the 20th century. Basie contributed
many innovative pieces to jazz history, such as
"One O'Clock Jump," "April in Paris," and
"Splanky." He was also the leader of one of the
most famous and longest-running jazz orchestras
in history, which collaborated with many
legendary singers and instrumentalists, such as
Billie Holiday, Lester Young, and Frank Sinatra.
He also introduced innovative arranging and
visual ideas into his performances, which further
increased his popularity and importance in the

music world. Basie has received nine Grammy Awards and numerous other awards and
honors and remains one of the most influential and beloved jazz musicians in history.

Count Basie was a member of 'Wisdom Lodge № 102' and 'Medina Lodge № 19' in New
York (within Prince Hall Freemasonry).

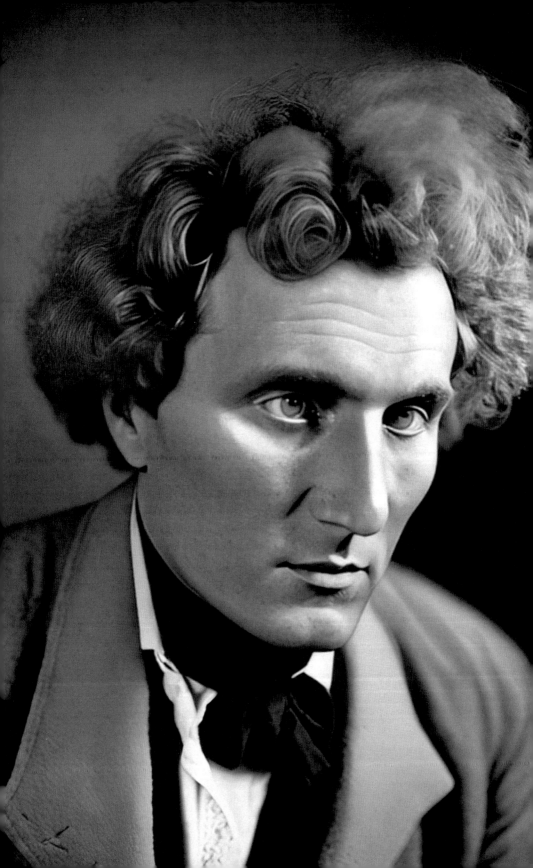

MARC CHAGALL

Color is all. When color is right, form is right.
Color is everything; color is vibration like music;
everything is vibration.

Marc Chagall

Marc Chagall (1887-1985) was a Russian-French artist who worked in many fields of art, such as painting, drawing, book illustration, stained glass, scenography, and ceramics. He created his unique style, which combined elements of Cubism, Expressionism, Surrealism, and folk art. Chagall's works reflected his personal experiences as a Jew from Belarus and his love for his wife, Bella. Chagall painted many well-known and highly regarded frescoes and stained-glass windows for churches and public institutions around the world. He received numerous awards and prizes for his work. He is considered one of the greatest artists of the 20th century.

Chagall was an active member of the 'Vitebsk' lodge belonging to the Grand Orient of the Peoples of Russia, from 1912.

SUGAR RAY ROBINSON

*To be a champ, you have to believe in yourself
when no one else will.*

Sugar Ray Robinson

Sugar Ray Robinson was an American professional boxer who is considered one of the best
boxers of all time. He was a six-time world
champion: once at welterweight (1946-1951)
and five times at middleweight (1951-1960),
going down in history as the first boxer to win
five world titles in the same category. His
fighting style combined speed, agility, and strength. He was known for his ability to adapt to
different opponents and situations. He contributed many spectacular fights to the fortunes of
the boxing world, such as the famous "Valen-
tine's Day Massacre" against Jake LaMotta or
the "fight of the century" against Carmen
Basilio. He also influenced popular culture, being the inspiration for the characters Rocky
Balboa and Raging Bull. Sugar Ray Robinson was not only a great athlete but also a social
activist and philanthropist. He established a foundation for needy children and supported
the civil rights movement.

Robinson belonged to Prince Hall Freemasonry and, while living in New York, attended
meetings of 'Joppa Lodge № 55'. His colleague Jack Dempsey was also a Freemason.

IRVING BERLIN

*Life is 10 percent what you make it
and 90 percent how you take it.*

Irving Berlin

Irving Berlin was an American composer and lyricist of Jewish descent who wrote nearly 1,500 songs. His music is an important part of the so-called Great American Songbook. He was born in Czarist Russia and came to the United States at the age of five. He contributed many unforgettable songs to the fortunes of the world of popular music, such as "White Christmas," "God Bless America," "There's No Business-Like Show Business," and "Puttin' on the Ritz." His songs were performed by many well-known artists, such as Bing Crosby, Fred Astaire, Judy Garland, and Ella Fitzgerald. He was also the creator of many popular musicals on Broadway and in Hollywood, such as "Annie Get Your Gun," "Top Hat" and "Easter Parade." Irving Berlin was not only an outstanding musician but also a patriot and humanist. He supported the American armed forces during both world wars and donated earnings from some of his songs to charity.

Berlin received his first three degrees of initiation at 'Munn Lodge № 190' in New York. He joined the Scottish Rite structures and became a Shriner.

Our Constitution works, our great republic is a government of laws and not of men. Here, the people rule.

Gerald R. Ford

Gerald Ford (1913-2006) was an American politician who served as the 38th President of the United States from 1974 to 1977. He was also an athlete and lawyer, playing American soccer in college and working as an attorney before embarking on a political career. He was the only President who was not elected to either the office or the vice presidency; he was nominated as vice president after Spiro Agnew resigned and assumed the presidential office after Richard Nixon stepped down over the Watergate scandal. He contributed many controversial decisions to the history of politics, such as pardoning Nixon, signing the Strategic Arms Limitation

Treaty with the USSR, beginning the process of normalizing relations with China, and evacuating US troops from South Vietnam. Ford's presidency was also marked by economic and energy crises and two failed attempts on his life.

Ford was initiated in 'Malta Lodge № 465'. He joined the Ancient and Accepted Scottish Rite and other Masonic organizations, including the Shriners.

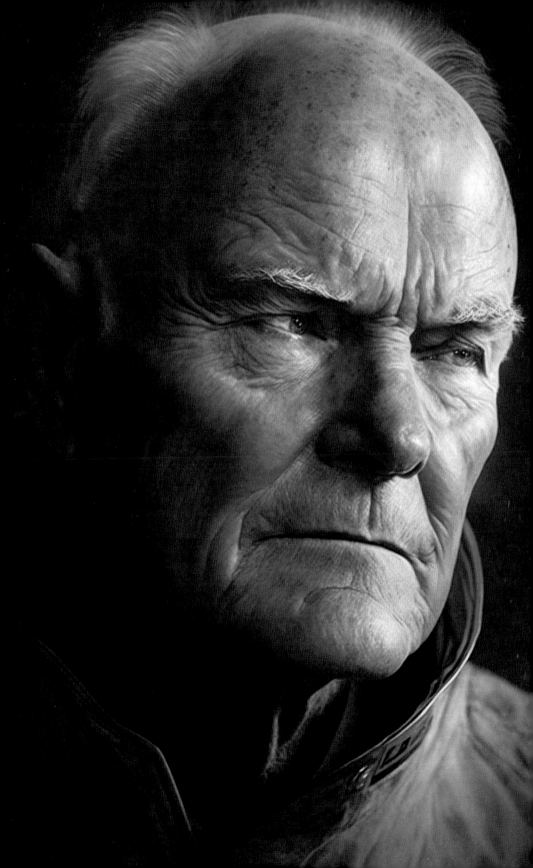

John Glenn (1921-2016) was an American aviator, astronaut, engineer, businessman, and politician. His contributions to world history are
many achievements in space exploration and
public service. He was the third American in
space and the first to orbit the Earth. He made
this historic flight on February 20, 1962, aboard
the Mercury 623 spacecraft. After his career as
an astronaut, he became a United States Senator
for the Democratic Party and represented the
state of Ohio for 25 years. In 1998, he flew into
space again at the age of seventy-seven as a crew
member of the shuttle Discovery and became the
oldest man in space. John Glenn was not only

a national hero but also a philanthropist. He founded the John Glenn College of Public
Affairs at Ohio State University and supported many charitable organizations. Glenn's flight
became a symbol of hope and achievement for the West during the Cold War and inspired
a new generation of young people to dream of a career in space.

*John Glenn petitioned for admission to 'Concord Lodge № 688' in his hometown of New
Concord, Ohio. However, a buildup of responsibilities meant that he could not receive
further degrees until 14 years later, in August 1978, when he was already an established
astronaut and senator. The ceremony for the conferring of the first three degrees took place
in the presence of three hundred Freemasons and was carried out "at sight ."Glenn later
progressed through the Scottish degrees, eventually receiving the 33rd degree of the
Ancient and Accepted Scottish Rite and honorary membership in the Supreme Council.
The 33rd-degree ring can be seen on his finger in photos taken of him when he returned
to space at the age of 77.*

SOURCES

Bibliographic clues confirming the Masonic affiliation of
the characters in this book.

JOHN LOCKE

Encyklopadie der Freimaurerei. Carl Lenning, Lipsk 1822–1828.

*

John Locke and Masonry: A Document. Claude E. Jones, Neuphilologische Mitteilungen Vol. 67, Nº 1 (1966).

JONATHAN SWIFT

Hitotsubashi Journal of Arts and Sciences 38 (1997) 13-22. C The Hitotsubashi Academy : *Jonathan Swift and Freemasonry* Katsumi Hashinuma: https://hermes-ir.lib.hit-u.ac.jp/hermes/ir/re/13309/HJart0380100130.pdf

*

Masonic biography on the Grand Lodge of British Columbia and Yukon website.: https://freemasonry.bcy.ca/biography/swift_j/swift_j.html

*

10,000 Famous Freemasons by William R.Denslow, Published by Macoy Publishing & Masonic Supply Co., Inc. Richmond, Virginia, 1957.

MONTESQUIEU

The Foundations of Modern Freemasonry: The Grand Architects. Berman, Ric (2012), Political Change and the Scientific Enlightenment, 1714–1740 (Eastbourne: Sussex Academic Press, 2012). Page 150.

*

Freemasonry and Education in Eighteenth Century France. Ian Cumming, History of Education Journal, Vol. 5, Nº 4 (Summer, 1954)

*

10,000 Famous Freemasons by William R.Denslow, Published by Macoy Publishing & Masonic Supply Co., Inc. Richmond, Virginia, 1957.

FRANCIS I

John Theophilus Desaguliers: A Natural Philosopher, Engineer and Freemason in Newtonian England. Audrey Carpenter, London, Continuum, 2011., ISBN 978-1-4411-2778-5, p. 47.

*

Wolnomularstwo w świetle encyklopedyj. Wypisy, Warsaw 1934, p. 6.

*

Results of studies of the Lodge Nº 2076 Quatuor Coronati: https://www.1723constitutions.com/the-context/politics-religion/the-duke-of-lorraine/

CLAUDE ADRIEN HELVETIUS

Wolnomularstwo w świetle encyklopedyj. Wypisy, Warsaw 1934, p. 7.

*

Helvetius: His Life and Place in the History of Educational Thought. Ian Cumming, Routledge, 2013, pp. 115–132.

*

In Search of Helvetius' Early Career as a Freemason. Gordon R. Silber, Eighteenth-Century Studies, Vol. 15, Nº 4 (Summer, 1982).

VOLTAIRE

The Freemasons: A History of the World's Most Powerful Secret Society. Jasper Ridley (2011). Skyhorse Publishing Inc. p. 141. ISBN 978-1-61145-010-1.

*

When Franklin Met Voltaire. Family Security Matters, Young, Adrian (19 July 2010). Archived from the original on 8 August 2020. Retrieved 25 June 2018.

*

In Search of Helvetius' Early Career as a Freemason. Gordon R. Silber, Eighteenth-Century Studies, Vol. 15, Nº 4 (Summer, 1982).

GOTTHOLD EPHRAIM LESSING

The Royal Masonic Cyclopaedia, Kenneth Mackenzie 1877. p. 205.

Ars Quatuor Coronatorum vol. 88 (1975) pp. 98-104. His lodge certificate (1771), currently located in the library of National Grand Lodge of Denmark (DDFO); See the reprint at Meddelelser fra Den Danske Frimurerorden ('Transactions' Nº 10, p.156) 1952.

*

Gotthold Ephraim Lessing. 2013. Grand Lodge of British Columbia and Yukon. Retrieved March 5, 2023.

JOHANN CHRISTIAN BACH

10,000 Famous Freemasons by William R.Denslow, Published by Macoy Publishing & Masonic Supply Co., Inc. Richmond, Virginia, 1957.

*

Masonic Allusions in the Dedications of Two Canons by J.S. Bach: BWV 1078 and 1075.

*

Bach Vol. 43, Nº 2 (2012), Mary Greer, ss. 1-45 (45 pages), Published By: Riemenschneider Bach Institute

FREDERICK II THE GREAT

A New Encyclopedia of Freemasonry, Waite, Arthur Edward (1994) [1921]. Volume I. New York: Wings Books. ISBN 978-0-517-19148-4. OCLC 777435960.

*

History of Frederick the Great: Comprehending a Complete History of the Silesian Campaigns and the Seven Years' War. Kugler, Franz Theodor (1845) [1840]. Translated by Moriarty, Edward Aubrey. Illustrated by Menzel, Adolph. London: Henry G. Bohn. OCLC 249507287.

*

The Rise of the Public in Enlightenment Europe. Melton, James Van Horn (2001). Cambridge,UK: Cambridge University Press. ISBN 978-0-521-46969-2. OCLC 1267424369.

*

History of Frederick the Great: Comprehending a Complete History of the Silesian Campaigns and the Seven Years' War. Kugler, Franz Theodor (1845) [1840]. Translated by Moriarty, Edward Aubrey. Illustrated by Menzel, Adolph. London: Henry G. Bohn. OCLC 249507287.

BENJAMIN FRANKLIN

Encyclopedia of Freemasonry, Mackey, Albert G., An, The Masonic History Company, Chicago, 1966.

*

10,000 Famous Freemasons by William R.Denslow, Published by Macoy Publishing & Masonic Supply Co., Inc. Richmond, Virginia, 1957.

*

The History Channel, *Mysteries of the Freemasons: America,* video documentary, August 1, 2006, written by Noah Nicholas and Molly Bedell.

*

The History and Collections of the Library Company of Philadelphia, Van Horne, John C. The Magazine Antiques, v. 170. № 2: 58–65 (1971).

*

Franklin, Benjamin (1706–1790). Lemay, Leo (2014) [2004]. Oxford Dictionary of National Biography (online ed.). Oxford University Press. doi:10.1093/ref:odnb/52466. (Subscription or UK library card required).

WOLFGANG AMADEUS MOZART

Mozart in Vienna. Braunbehrens, Volkmar (1990). New York: Grove and Weidenfeld.

*

Mozart: A Documentary Biography. Deutsch, Otto Erich (1965). Stanford: Stanford University Press.

*

Mozart: A Life. Solomon, Maynard (1995). HarperCollins.

*

The Masonic Thread in Mozart. Thomson, Katherine (1977). London: Lawrence and Wishart. ISBN 0853153817.

*

Mozart and the Enlightenment, Till, Nicholas (1992). London: Faber.

ROBERT BURNS

Robert Burns and his world. Daiches, David. New York: Viking Press, 1971.

*

The Near Miss of Robert Burns: Why the Caledonian Poet was not a Calypso Balladeer in The Scottish Rite Journal, Fox, William L. January 1998.

*

A Biography of Robert Burns. Mackay, James. Edinburgh: Mainstream Publishing, 1992.

*

Robert Burns in The Quest For Light, McLeod, Wallace..

*

Melbourne: Australia and New Zealand Masonic Research Council, 1997.

*

The Universality of Freemasonry in The Quest For Light, Tony Pope, ed.

*

Auld Lang Syne and Brother Robert Burns in The Scottish Rite Journal January 1997, Paterson, T.G. (http://www.srmason-sj.org/council/journal/1-jan/paterson.htm)

*

Burns and the Masonic Enlightenment in Aberdeen and the Enlightenment. Roberts, Marie. Aberdeen University Press, 1987.

JACQUES MONTGOLFIER

Wolnomularstwo w świetle encyklopedyj. Wypisy, Warsaw 1934, p. 7.

*

Dictionnaire de la Franc-Maçonnerie (Daniel Ligou, Presses Universitaires de France, 2006).

*

American Mason. Andrew Boracci, ed.. Sag Harbor, NY. 1997.

*

10,000 Famous Freemasons by William R.Denslow, Published by Macoy Publishing & Masonic Supply Co., Inc. Richmond, Virginia, 1957.

GEORGE WASHINGTON

Washington: A Life. Penguin Press. ISBN 978-1594202667.

*

George Washington: A Life. Randall, Willard Sterne (1997). Henry Holt & Co. ISBN 978-0805027792.

*

Freemasonry. George Washington's Mount Vernon. Immekus, Alexander (2018). Mount Vernon Ladies' Association. Retrieved March 5, 2023.

ERASMUS DARWIN

10,000 Famous Freemasons by William R.Denslow, Published by Macoy Publishing & Masonic Supply Co., Inc. Richmond, Virginia, 1957.

*

For Mother Lodge cf. H. L. Haywood, Supplement *Mackey Encyclopedia of Freemasonry.* 1966. s. 1198.

*

Erasmus Darwin. Grand Lodge of British Columbia and Yukon. Retrieved March 3, 2023.

HORATIO NELSON

Nelson and His 'Band of Brothers': Friendship, Freemasonry, Fraternity. Martyn Downer, ss 30–48/ Palgrave Macmillan

*

William R. Denslow, 10,000 Famous Freemasons. ss. 258-59. Lodge number should be 236.

*

Horatio Admiral Lord Nelson, Was He a ... Mason? John Webb, Hersham : Ian Allan Lewis Masonic, 1998. pp. 35-39;

*

History of Freemasonry in Norfolk, Hamon Le Strange.

PRINCE HALL

Inside Prince Hall. David L. Gray, Lancaster, Virginia: Anchor Communications LLC, 2004.

*

All Men Free and Brethren: Essays on the History of African American Freemasonry, Peter s. Hinks and Stephen Kantrowitz (eds.). Ithaca, NY: Cornell University Press, 2013.

*

The Bucks of America & Prince Hall Freemasonry, Gregory S. Kearse, Prince Hall Masonic Digest Newspaper, (Washington, D.C. 2012), 8.

*

Out of the Shadows: Prince Hall Freemasonry in America, 200 Years of Endurance. Alton G. Roundtree and Paul M. Bessel, Forestville MD: KLR Publishing, 2006. [ISBN missing]

*

The National Grand Lodge and Prince Hall Freemasonry: The Untold Truth. Alton G. Roundtree, Forestville MD: KLR Publishing, 2010.

FRANZ JOSEPH HAYDN

1785 - The Year Haydn, Mozart & Freemasonry were the news, https://www.fjhaydn.com/my-blog/2015/03/1785-the-year-.html

*

10,000 Famous Freemasons by William R.Denslow, Published by Macoy Publishing & Masonic Supply Co., Inc. Richmond, Virginia, 1957.

*

Mozart in Vienna. Braunbehrens, Volkmar (1990). New York: Grove and Weidenfeld.

JOHANN GOTTLIEB FICHTE

Kleine Werklehre der Freimaurerei. I. Das Buch des Lehrlings. Imhof, Gottlieb (1959). 5th ed. Lausanne: Alpina, s. 42.

*

Fichte und die hermetische Demokratie der Freimaurer. Lawatsch, Hans-Helmut (1991). In: Hammacher, Klaus, Schottky, Richard, Schrader, Wolfgang H. and Daniel Breazeale (eds.).

*

Sozialphilosophie. Fichte-Studien, Vol. 3. Amsterdam-Atlanta: Editions Rodopi, s. 204, ISBN 978-90-5183-236-5.

*

To read more about the role of Freemasonry in Fichte's trip to Jena, see: Klaus Hammacher, *Fichte und die Freimaurerei'*, in Fichte-Studien 2/1990, ss. 138-159; Hans-Helmut Lawatsch, *Fichte und die hermetische Demokratie der Freimaurei'*, in Fichte-Studien, 3/1991, pp. 204-218.

*

Fichte as a Freemason: October 1872 to September 1873. Albert G. Mackey, ed. (2003). Mackey's National Freemason. p. 430. ISBN 978-0-7661-5717-0.

*

Hegel and the Hermetic Tradition, Glenn Alexander Magee, Cornell University Press, 2008, p. 55.

JAMES WATT

Famous Scottish Freemasons. The Grand Lodge of Antient Free and Accepted Masons of Scotland. 2010. pp.72–73. ISBN 978-0-9560933-8-7

*

James Watt. 2013. Grand Lodge of British Columbia and Yukon. Retrieved March 5, 2023.

*

James Watt's Masonic certificate: transcription: https://www.researchgate.net/figure/Brother-James-Watts-1736-1818-masonic-certificate-Transcription_fig3_271071868

EDWARD JENNER

Jenner was the subject of an article in the official periodical of the United Grand Lodge of England Freemasonry Today in 2010. www.freemasonrytoday.com/news/lodges-chapters-a-individuals/item/238-edward-jenner-freemason-and-natural-philosopher

*

ARS Quatuor Coronatorum, AQC Vol. 104.

*

Edward Jenner. 2013. Grand Lodge of British Columbia and Yukon. Retrieved March 5, 2023.

TSAR ALEXANDER I

Freemasonry in Russia: The Grand Lodge of Astraea (1815-1822). Lauren G. Leighton, The Slavonic and East European Review, Vol. 60, Nº 2 (Apr., 1982), pp. 244-261.

*

Russian Tsar Freemasons , IK-PTZ, https://ik-ptz.ru/en/exam-tests---2016-social-studies/russkie-cari-masony-rossiya-pod-vlastyu-masonov-glaz-v-piramide.html

SIMON BOLIVAR

Simon Bolivar, the Latin American Liberator and Freemasonry. Melvin E.Silverio, The Freemason Magazine, March 2019.

*

The Freemason Simón Bolívar between myth and historical truth. Ferrer Benimeli, José Antonio. REHMLAC [online]. 2020, vol.12, n.1-2, ss.1-34. ISSN 1659-4223. http://dx.doi.org/10.15517/rehmlac.v12i1-2.40744.

*

Simon Bolivar, Freemason, by Bro. F. W. Seal-Coon, (Norman B. Spencer Award 1977), https://www.1723constitutions.com/wp-content/uploads/2021/01/AQC-90-1977-Sirnon-Bolivar-Freemason.pdf (Quator Coronati).

JAMES MONROE

Monroe, James. Mason, Soldier, Statesman. by Gilbert H. Hill. https://www.knightstemplar.org/KnightTemplar/articles/JamesMonroe.htm

*

How many US presidents were Freemasons? https://museumfreemasonry.org.uk/blog/learn-about-freemasonry-how-many-us-presidents-were-freemasons (UGLE official website)

*

Le petit dictionnaire des (vrais et faux) frères. Alain Bauer, Roger Dachez. Flammarion, p. 133.

SIR WALTER SCOTT

Sir Walter Scott as a freemason, Adam Muir Mackay. Ars Quatuor Coronatorum,vol xx (1907) pp. 209-20. Also see The Masonic Tidings, January, 1911: Milwaukee, Wisconsin. p. 7.

*

Sir Walter Scott and Freemasonry. Dudley Wright, http://phoenixmasonry.org/sir_walter_scott_and_freemasonry.htm

*

The Masonic Tidings, January, 1911: Milwaukee, Wisconsin. p. 7.

JOHANN WOLFGANG VON GOETHE

Recasting Cosmopolitanism: German Freemasonry and Regional Identity in the Early Nineteenth Century. Beachy, Robert (2000). Eighteenth-Century Studies. 33 (2): 266–274. doi:10.1353/ecs.2000.0002. JSTOR 30053687. S2CID 162003813.

*

Die Mitglieder des Illuminatenordens, 1776 1787/93. Schüttler, Hermann (1991). Munich: Ars Una. pp. 48–49, 62-63, 71, 82. ISBN 978-3-89391-018-2.

The Story of Civilization Volume 10: Rousseau and Revolution. Will Durant (1967). Simon&Schuster. p. 607.

PEDRO I

Freemasonry in Brazil, William de Carvalho's, published in Ars Quatuor Coronatorum 124 (2011): https://www.1723constitutions.com/wp-content/uploads/2021/01/William-de-Carvalho-Freemasonry-in-Brazil-AQC-124-2011.pdf

Freemasonry in Brazil (Ninetentch Century): History and sociability. Alexandre Mansur Barata, 2013, Universitad de Costarica: file:///C:/Users/User/Desktop/do_kas/Dialnet-FreemasonryInBrazilNineteenthCentury-5285148.pdf

ALEXANDER PUSHKIN

Freemasonry : A Celebration of the Craft. Hamill, John et al. JG Press 1998. ISBN:1572152672.

BERNARDO O' HIGGINS

The Lautaro Lodges. Keld J. Reynolds, The Americas. Vol. 24, Nº 1 (Jul., 1967), ss. 18-32 (15 pages), published by Cambridge University Press.

L'Amérique latine et la Caraïbe des Lumières, collective work under the direction of Alain de Keghel, Dervy, Paris 2017.

JAMES KNOX POLK

James Knox Polk A Famous Freemason. Paperback – September 10, 2010, by George W. Baird. Kessinger Legacy Reprints.

Le petit dictionnaire des (vrais et faux) frères. Alain Bauer, Roger Dachez. Flammarion, p. 137.

JOSE DE SAN MARTIN

Seamos libres y lo demás no importa nada [Let us be free and nothing else matters] (in Spanish). Galasso, Norberto (2000). Buenos Aires: Colihue. ISBN 978-950-581-779-5.

L'Amérique latine et la Caraïbe des Lumières, collective work under the direction of Alain de Keghel, Dervy, Paris 2017.

LORD WELLINGTON

Ars Quatuor Coronatorum. Vol. xv, 1902, p. 108-124. note p. 117.

*

Wellington: Soldier, Politician and Initiated Freemason, by W.Bro. Yasha Beresiner, [see brief biographical note after the lecture], Past Master (1997/8), Quatuor Coronati Lodge No 2076 (Premier Lodge of Masonic Research). http://www.irishmasonichistory.com/wellington-soldier-politician-and-initiated-freemason-by-wbro-yasha-beresiner.html

SAMUEL COLT

Colt Joins the Craft, AASR Valley of Boston: https://scottishriteboston.com/en/article_view.php?news_id=850#.ZAMUU3bMKbh

*

Masonrytoday.com: *Samuel Colt passes away:* https://www.masonrytoday.com/index.php?new_month=1&new_day=10&new_year=2015

*

10,000 Famous Freemasons by William R.Denslow, Published by Macoy Publishing & Masonic Supply Co., Inc. Richmond, Virginia, 1957.

PIERRE JOSEPH PROUDHON

P.-J. Proudhon et la Franc-maçonnerie : documents publiés à l'occasion de l'inauguration de sa statue, 14 août 1910 / Dr. Ant. Magnin

*

Pierre Joseph Proudhon et la Franc-Maçonnerie. André Combes. In a Masonic periodical of the Grand Orient of France Humanisme 2009/2 (N° 285), pages from 87 to 95.

GIUSEPPE MAZZINI

10,000 Famous Freemasons by William R.Denslow, Published by Macoy Publishing & Masonic Supply Co., Inc. Richmond, Virginia, 1957.

*

A Cosmopolitanism of Nations: Giuseppe Mazzini's Writingson Democracy, Nation Building, and International Relations, Stefano Recchia and Nadia Urbinati, eds. (Princeton, N.J.: Princeton University Press).

BENITO JUAREZ

Freemasonry. Karen Racine, in Michael S. Werner, ed Encyclopedia of Mexico (1997) p. 1:540.

*

Masonic biography on the official website of the mixed freemasonry Le Droit Humain: https://www.
universalfreemasonry.org/en/famous-freemasons/benito-juarez

*

L'Amérique latine et la Caraïbe des Lumières, collective work under the direction of Alain de Keghel, Dervy,
Paris 2017.

JULES FRANCOIS SIMON

Jules Simon (1814-1896). Philosophie, laïcité et liberté. Bibliothèque de l'Institut, 2015: https://www.
bibliotheque-institutdefrance.fr/sites/default/files/jules_simon_catalogue_dexpo.pdf

*

*Les francs-maçons et la laïcisation de l'école. Mythe et réalités (The Freemasons and the Laicization of School. Myth
and Realities).* Jean-Paul Delahaye. Histoire de'l Education, 109 | 2006

*

Filozofia masonerii (Philosophy of Freemasonry). Andrzej Nowicki, 2022, Warsaw.

GIUSEPPE GARIBALDI

Giuseppe Garibaldi Massone. "Giuseppe Garibaldi" lodges meeting and study conference. Report of Grand
Master Gustavo Raffi. Grand Orient of Italy of Palazzo Giustiniani, Via di San Pancrazio, 8 - 00152 Roma.
Trieste - October 26, 2002.

*

Autobiography of Giuseppe Garibaldi. A. Werner, Vol. III, Howard Fertig, New York (1971) p. 68.

LOUIS BLANC

Proudhon. Denis William Brogan, London, H. Hamilton, 1934. chapter iv; Henri du Bac. Prodhon et le
Christianisme (1945) [The Un-Marxian Socialist. A Study of Proudhon]. Henri de Lubac S. J. Translated by
R. E. Scantlebury. New York: Sheed & Ward, 1948. ss. xvi, p. 304.

*

Freemasonry and nineteenth-century revolution, https://freemasonry.bcy.ca/history/revolution/index.html#14

*

Filozofia masonerii (Philosophy of Freemasonry). Andrzej Nowicki, 2022, Warsaw.

LEON GAMBETTA

Les Frères en Lutte? Provincial Freemasonry on the Eve of the Third Republic. Vincent Wright, French
Politics and Society, Vol. 9, Nº 2 (Spring 1991), pp. 39-52 (14 pages). Published By: Berghahn Books.

*

*

Republicanism and Utopian Vision: French Freemasonry in the 1860s and 1870s. Philip Nord, The Journal of Modern History, Vol. 63, N° 2, A Special Issue on Modern France (Jun., 1991), ss. 213-229 (17 pages). Published By: The University of Chicago Press.

FRANZ LISZT
Ars Quatuor Coronatorum, London : Quatuor Coronati Lodge N° 2076, 2011.
*

Franz Liszt. Huneker, James (1911). New York: Charles Scribner's Sons.
*

Fr. Liszt Porträt. Lipsius Klinkuht Musik Wesenberg St. Petersburg 1886.

WILLIAM I
William I, German Emperor, biography: https://www.dafato.com/en/history/biographies/william-i,-german-emperor.
*

Photo of William I wearing Masonic regalia:
https://wolnomularstwo.pl/wp-content/uploads/2016/08/znanimasoni2-211x300.jpg
*

VICTOR SCHOELCHER
Victor Schoelcher, républicain et franc-maçon. Anne Girollet, Edimaf, 2000.
*

Filozofia masonerii (Philosophy of Freemasonry). Andrzej Nowicki, 2022, Warsaw.
*

Le petit dictionnaire des (vrais et faux) frères. Alain Bauer, Roger Dachez. Flammarion, pp. 143-144.

OSCAR WILDE
Oscar Wilde - A University Mason. Yasha Beresiner, Quatuor Coronati Lodge No 2076 (Premier Lodge of Masonic Research) : http://www.irishmasonichistory.com/oscar-wilde-freemason.html

WILLIAM MCKINLNEY
Major McKinley: William McKinley and the Civil War. Armstrong, William H. (2000). Kent, Ohio: The Kent State University Press. ISBN 978-0-87338-657-9.

William McKinley: President and Freemason. Scottish Rite Maxonic Museum & Library:
https://www.srmml.org/exhibitions/past-exhibitions/2020-past-exhibitions/william-mckinley-president-and-freemason/

*

Museum of Freemasonry (UGLE): https://museumfreemasonry.org.uk/blog/learn-about-freemasonry-how-many-us-presidents-were-freemasons

SWAMI VIVEKANANDA

Masonic biography on the Grand Lodge of British Columbia and Yukon website.
https://freemasonry.bcy.ca/biography/vivekananda/vivekananda.html

*

The Telegraph newspaper edition, Calcutta, India. Sunday, May 09, 2004.

FREDERIC A. BARTHOLDI

The Statue of Liberty. Moreno, Barry (10 November 2004). Arcadia Publishing. ISBN 978-1-4396-3220-8.

*

Massoni Famosi. Giuseppe Seganti, Rome, Atanòr, 2005, ISBN 88-7169-223-3.
Hamill, John et al.. Freemasonry : A Celebration of the Craft. JG Press 1998. ISBN:1572152672.

MARK TWAIN

Mark Twain and Freemasonry. Alexander E. Jones, American Literature. Vol. 26, N° 3 (Nov., 1954), pp. 363-373 (11 pages), Published By: Duke University Press.

*

Tales from Masonic pen, discovering the fraternal life of Mark Twain, by Heather Boerner.

EDWARD VII

King Edward VII – A Monarch and a Freemason:
https://freemasonrymatters.co.uk/index.php/king-edward-vii-a-monarch-and-a-freemason/

*

Encyclopedia of Freemasonry. Albert G. Mackey, p. 315.

*

10,000 Famous Freemasons by William R.Denslow, Published by Macoy Publishing & Masonic Supply Co., Inc. Richmond, Virginia, 1957.

*

Le petit dictionnaire des (vrais et faux) frères. Alain Bauer, Roger Dachez. Flammarion. p. 114.

JEAN HENRI DUNANT

Henry Dunant Franc-Macon? Roger Durand: https://www.shd.ch/docs/SHD_Bulletin21a.pdf

*

10,000 Famous Freemasons by William R.Denslow, Published by Macoy Publishing & Masonic Supply Co., Inc. Richmond, Virginia, 1957.

EDWARD ABRAMOWSKI

Wschód Wielkiego Wschodu. Wojciech Giełżyński, Warsaw 2008.

*

Filozofia masonerii (Philosophy of Freemasonry). Andrzej Nowicki, Warsaw 2022.

*

Masoneria polska XX wieku (Polish Freemasonry of the 20th century). Ludwik Hass, Warsaw 1996, p. 41-43, 157.

THEODORE ROOSEVELT

Theodore Roosevelt. mdmasons.org. The Grand Lodge of Maryland. Archived from the original on November 16, 2020. Retrieved March 5, 2023.

*

Le petit dictionnaire des (vrais et faux) frères. Alain Bauer, Roger Dachez. Flammarion. p. 188.

JUAN GRIS

Dictionnaire des Francs-Maçons. Michel Gaudart de Soulages and Hubert Lamant (Paris, J. C. Lattès, 1995).

*

Juan Gris: du Bateau-Lavoir à la rue Cadet. Pascal Bajou, La Chaîne d'Union, Revue d'études symboliques et maçonniques de Grand Orient de France, Nouvelle Série, Numéro 20 [Printemps 2002], pp. 63–77; pp. 69 and 72 and 73).

*

Juan Gris à Boulogne. Emmanuel Bréon, (Paris, Herscher, 1992).

*

Masonic passport and other documents reproduced by José A. García-Diego, Antonio Machado y Juan Gris, in *Dos artistas masones* (Madrid, Editorial Castalia, 1990).

ERNEST SHACKLETON

Sir Ernest Shackleton on the webpage of the United Grand Lodge of England: https://www.ugle.org.uk/discover-freemasonry/famous-freemasons/sir-ernest-shackleton

*

The Navy Lodge Nº 2612, The First Hundred Years by W Bro Captain D.M. Swain, Royal Navy, 2004.

HARRY HOUDINI

Famous Freemason: Harry Houdini. Ancient Accepted Scottish Rite. Valley of Boston:
https://www.scottishriteboston.net/en/article_view.php?news_id=802#.ZAM9vHbMKbg

*

Harry Houdini, The Grand Lodge of Ohio: https://www.freemason.com/harry-houdini/

WILLIAM HOWARD TAFT

Le petit dictionnaire des (vrais et faux) frères. Alain Bauer, Roger Dachez. Flammarion, p. 191.

*

President William Howard Taft's Trowel: spreading the cementing of unity and tolerance in public health. Jonathan
Kopel. J Community Hosp Intern Med Perspect. 2021; 11(6): 880–886. Published online 2021 Nov 15. doi:
10.1080/20009666.2021.1983979

ARTHUR CONAN DOYLE

Arthur Conan Doyle, Spiritualist and Freemason. Yasha Beresiner, Masonic papers. Pietre-Stones Review of
Freemasonry. Retrieved Marh 4, 2023. http://www.freemasons-freemasonry.com/beresiner10.html

*

Arthur Conan Doyle - on the webpage of the United Grand Lodge of England:
https://www.ugle.org.uk/discover-freemasonry/famous-freemasons/arthur-conan-doyle

JOSEPH JOFFRE

Le général Joffre, génie militaire. Thomas Hofnung, Liberation, August 3, 2014:
https://www.liberation.fr/planete/2014/08/03/le-general-joffre-genie-militaire_1075024/

*

Le petit dictionnaire des (vrais et faux) frères. Alain Bauer, Roger Dachez. Flammarion, p. 175.

SIR THOMAS LIPTON

Famous men members of Masonic Lodges. American Canadian Grand Lodge ACGL. Retrieved November 17,
2018.

*

Famous members of Masonic Lodges. Bavaria Lodge Nº 935 A.F. & A. M. Retrieved October 18, 2018.

*

List of Famous Masons in the history. Highland Lodge No 762 F& A. M. Fort Wayne IN. Retrieved November
9, 2014.

*

Famous Freemasons in the course of history. St. John Lodge No 11 F.A.A.M. Archived from the original on 16 November 2015. Retrieved 30 September 2018.

*

Masonic biography on the Grand Lodge of British Columbia and Yukon website: https://freemasonry.bcy.ca/biography/lipton_t/lipton_t.html

JOHN PHILIP SOUSA

Biography of John Philip Sousa. Paul E. Bierley (October 28, 1997). Scottish Rite Journal. Archived from the original on November 6, 2005. Paul E. Bierley is a member of Whitehall Nº 761, Whitehall, Ohio.

*

John Philip Sousa, Band Leader, Dies in Hotel at Reading. (special edition). The New York Times. March 6, 1932. Retrieved August 25, 2018.

KING CAMP GILETTE

Trowel, Boston: Grand Lodge of Masons in Massachusetts, Summer 2003, vol. 21, Nº 2: p. 22.

ANNIE BESANT

A short biography of Dr. Annie Besant, Curuppumullage Jinarajadasa (1877-1953) pp. 43-45. Adyar : Vosanta Press, 1932. pp. 73. ; 80.

*

A brief history of the founding of Co-Freemasonry, A lecture given at Canonbury Masonic Research Centre on 27 September 1999 by Jeanne Heaslewood.

ANDRE CITROEN

Frère Citroën, vous avez la parole..., Philippe Benhamou, in Collectif, Citroën et les arts, 2013, Fage Editions, p.38.

*

Le petit dictionnaire des (vrais et faux) frères. Alain Bauer, Roger Dachez. Flammarion, p. 165.

RUDYARD KIPLING

Encyclopedia of Freemasonry, Vol. 1. Mackey, Albert G. (1946). Chicago: The Masonic History Co.

*

Our brother Rudyard Kipling. Masonic Lecture archived on March 8, 2012. Albertpike.wordpress.com (7 października 2011 r.). Retrieved May 4, 2017.

*

Official Visit to Meridian Lodge №̲ 687 (PDF). 12 February 2014: https://www.hamiltondistrictcmasons.org/upload/lecture_file111.pdf

*

Kipling the Freemason. The Square Magazine: https://www.thesquaremagazine.com/mag/article/202005kipling-the-freemason/

KEMAL ATATURK

The History of Freemasonry In Turkey. Celil Layiktez. Pietre-Stones Review of Freemasonry.

*

Universal Freemasonry (Co-Masonry) Masonic Biographies: Mustafa Kemal Atatürk: https://www.universalfreemasonry.org/en/famous-freemasons/mustafa-ataturk

*

Freemasonry in the Ottoman Empire: A History of the Fraternity and its Influence in Syria and the Levant by Dorothe Sommer.

ALPHONSE MUCHA

Tajné společenství v Čechách – zednáři [Secret society in the Czech Republic – Freemasons]. ČT24. December 30, 2009 r. Retrieved January 25, 2011.

*

Prague.eu The official tourist site of Prague: https://www.prague.eu/en/object/places/3922/in-the-footsteps-of-alphonse-mucha-mucha-and-freemasonry-husova-street-9?back=1

*

A portrait of Alfonso Mucha in Masonic regalia: http://www.muchafoundation.org/en/gallery/browse-works/object/9

*

Le petit dictionnaire des (vrais et faux) frères. Alain Bauer, Roger Dachez. Flammarion, p. 185.

JANUSZ KORCZAK

An article about Janusz Korczak on the website of the Polish Prometea Lodge of the Grand Lodge of Women of France:

http://www.lozaprometea.pl/index.php/janusz-korczak-droga-do-wolnomularstwa

A copy of this article can be found at: https://gloria.tv/post/B3TMWUX3Jwwp4Lh4zQ3j8siC9

HENRI LA FONTAINE

The 100th anniversary of a Nobel Peace Prize. Henri La Fontaine (1854-1943), Nobel Peace Prize in 1913: https://artsandculture.google.com/story/NAXRQ5-erR8A8A

FRANKLIN DELANO ROOSEVELT

Franklin Delano Roosevelt - article on the webpage of the United Grand Lodge of England: https://museumfreemasonry.org.uk/blog/learn-about-freemasonry-how-many-us-presidents-were-freemasons

*

Masonic Encyclopedia: https://masonicshos.com/famous-freemasons/mason/?i=755

*

Famous Masons. MWGLNY. January 2014. Retrieved March 5, 2023.

*

10,000 Famous Freemasons by William R.Denslow, Published by Macoy Publishing & Masonic Supply Co., Inc. Richmond, Virginia, 1957.

HENRY FORD

Henry Ford - American Mason, Sag Harbor, NY. Aug/Dec 2001 p. 22

*

10,000 Famous Freemasons by William R.Denslow, Published by Macoy Publishing & Masonic Supply Co., Inc. Richmond, Virginia, 1957.

JOHN PERSHING

Freemasonry: A Celebration of the Craft. Hamill, John et al. JG Press 1998. ISBN 1-57215-267-2.

Le petit dictionnaire des (vrais et faux) frères. Alain Bauer, Roger Dachez. Flammarion, s. 185

GEORGE VI

George VI - article on the webpage of the United Grand Lodge of England: https://www.ugle.org.uk/discover-freemasonry/famous-freemasons/king-george-vi

*

Le petit dictionnaire des (vrais et faux) frères. Alain Bauer, Roger Dachez. Flammarion, p. 170.

ALEXANDER FLEMING

Alexander Fleming - article on the webpage of the United Grand Lodge of England: https://www.ugle.org.uk/discover-freemasonry/famous-freemasons/sir-alexander-fleming

*

Le petit dictionnaire des (vrais et faux) frères. Alain Bauer, Roger Dachez. Flammarion, p. 169.

JEAN SIBELIUS

Music for Freemasonry. Jean Sibelius. Finnish Club of Helsinki. Dostęp 04 March 2023.https://www.sibelius.
info/english/musiikki/vapaamuurari.htm

*

Le petit dictionnaire des (vrais et faux) frères. Alain Bauer, Roger Dachez. Flammarion, p. 190.

LOUIS B. MAYER

Today in Masonic History: Louis Burt Mayer passes away in 1957 (MasonryToday.com): https://www.
masonrytoday.com/index.php?new_month=10&new_day=29&new_year=2018

CECIL DE MILLE

Masonic biography on the Grand Lodge of British Columbia and Yukon website: https://freemasonry.bcy.
ca/biography/demille_c/demille_c.html

*

Today in Masonic History: Cecil de Mille passes away. Archived from the original on March 5, 2023.

ICHIRO HATOYAMA

Today in Masonic History Ichirō Hatoyama passes away in 1959: http://www.masonrytoday.com/index.
php?new_month=3&new_day=7&new_year=2016

*

Ichirō Hatoyama - article in Free Social Encyclopedia for the World: https://alchetron.com/Ichiro-
Hatoyama.

GEORGE MARSHAL

Made a Mason at Sight. Stewart, Greg (June 13, 2011). Masonic Education and Analysis. Freemason
Information. Archived from the original on February 6, 2015. Retrieved April 8, 2021.

*

Le petit dictionnaire des (vrais et faux) frères. Alain Bauer, Roger Dachez. Flammarion, ss. 180-181.

CLARK GABLE

Today in Masonic History. William Clark Gable is born 1901.
https://www.masonrytoday.com/index.php?new_month=2&new_day=1&new_year=2015

*

Clark Gable. Hollywood Actor. Freemason. Mutiny on the Bounty. by Travis Simpkins: http://www.tsimpkins. com/2021/02/clark-gable-hollywood-actor-freemason.html

DOUGLAS MACARTHUR

Herbert G. Gardiner, PGS, Grand Lodge of Hawaii F & A.M . http://www.calodges.org/ncrl/MACARTHU.htm

*

Masonic biography on the Grand Lodge of British Columbia and Yukon website: https://freemasonry.bcy.ca/biography/macarthur_d/macarthur_d.html

WINSTON CHURCHILL

Winston Churchil - article on the webpage of the United Grand Lodge of England: https://www.ugle.org.uk/discover-freemasonry/famous-freemasons/winston-churchill

*

Masonic biography on the official website of the mixed freemasonry Le Droit Humain:Winston Churchill: https://www.universalfreemasonry.org/en/famous-freemasons/winston-churchill

*

10,000 Famous Freemasons by William R.Denslow, Published by Macoy Publishing & Masonic Supply Co., Inc. Richmond, Virginia, 1957.

NAT KING COLE

Famous Freemason: *Nat King Cole's "Unforgettable" Escape*: http://www.midnightfreemasons.org/2012/02/famous-freemason-nat-king-cole-escape_03.html

*

The secret history of the jazz greats who were freemasons, John Lewis, The Guardian, July 2, 2016: https://www. theguardian.com/music/2014/jul/02/secret-jazz-freemason-history-duke-ellington-sun-ra

CAMILLE HYUSMANS

Camille Huysmans on the official website of the Grand Orient of Belgium: https://gob.be/team/huysmans-camille/

*

Socialisme et franc-maçonnerie. Le tournant du siècle (1880-1920). Denis Lefebvre,Paris, Bruno Leprince Éditeur, 2000.

JOHN STEINBECK

Masonic biography on the Grand Lodge of British Columbia and Yukon website: https://freemasonry.bcy.ca/biography/steinbeck_j/steinbeck_j.html

HARRY TRUMAN

Masonic biography on the Grand Lodge of British Columbia and Yukon website:
https://freemasonry.bcy.ca/biography/truman_h/truman_h.html

*

10,000 Famous Freemasons by William R.Denslow, Published by Macoy Publishing & Masonic Supply Co., Inc. Richmond, Virginia, 1957.

*

Grandview Masonic Lodge 618. Harry S. Truman Library and Museum. Independence, MO: National Archives and Records Administration. Retrieved June 28, 2022.

*

Harry Truman - article on the webpage of the United Grand Lodge of England: https://museumfreemasonry.org.uk/blog/learn-about-freemasonry-how-many-us-presidents-were-freemasons

LYNDON B. JOHNSON

Today in Masonic History Lyndon Baines Johnson was born in 1908:
http://www.masonrytoday.com/index.php?new_month=8&new_day=27&new_year=2021

*

Le petit dictionnaire des (vrais et faux) frères. Alain Bauer, Roger Dachez. Flammarion, pp. 175-176 Bauer.

*

Lyndon Baines Johnson - article on the webpage of the United Grand Lodge of England: https://museumfreemasonry.org.uk/blog/learn-about-freemasonry-how-many-us-presidents-were-freemasons

SALVADORE ALLENDE

The Chilean Revolution, Conversations with Allende. Régis Debray. New York : Vintage Books A Division of Random House, 1971. ISBN : 0-394-71726-0. 201 ss. 11 cm. x 18.5 cm. pp. 64-65, endnote pp. 136-37.

*

Masonic biography on the Grand Lodge of British Columbia and Yukon website:
https://freemasonry.bcy.ca/biography/allende_s/revolution.html

*

Famous Freemasons Masonic Presidents. Calodges.org. Archived from the original on 2 August 2008. Retrieved January 12, 2010.

DUKE ELLINGTON

The secret history of the jazz greats who were freemasons, John Lewis, The Guardian, July 2, 2016:
https://www.theguardian.com/music/2014/jul/02/secret-jazz-freemason-history-duke-ellington-sun-ra

*

Masonic biography on the official website of the mixed Freemasonry Le Droit Humain: https://www.universalfreemasonry.org/en/famous-freemasons/duke-ellington

VANNEVAR BUSH

Masonic biography on the Grand Lodge of British Columbia and Yukon website: https://freemasonry.bcy.ca/biography/bush_v/bush_v.html

*

10,000 Famous Freemasons by William R.Denslow, Published by Macoy Publishing & Masonic Supply Co., Inc. Richmond, Virginia, 1957.

CHARLES LINBERGH

Information on the website of the Scottish Rite Journal, reporting to the Grand Lodge of Maryland (Grand Lodge of Maryland): https://mdmasons.org/about-md-masons/famous-masons/charles-lindbergh/

*

Charles Lindbergh - Masonic Encyclopedia entry on the site: https://masonicshop.com/famous-freemasons/mason/?i=753

JOSEPHINE BAKER

Joséphine Baker « panthéonisée » était aussi franc-maçonne ! (audio)
https://www.frequenceterre.com/2021/11/27/josephine-baker-pantheonisee-etait-aussi-franc-maconne/

*

Masonic initiation of Josephine Baker (video): https://voix-libre.fr/josephine-baker-franc-maconne/

*

Les Franc-Maçonnes célèbres (website of the Grand Women Lodge of Cameroun)
https://glfcam.org/les-franc-maconnes-celebres/

*

Universal Freemasonry (Le Droit Humain Co-Masonry) Masonic Quotes: The Quotes of Josephine Baker: https://www.universalfreemasonry.org/en/freemason-quotes/josephine-baker

JACK WARNER

Today in Masonic History Jack Leonard "J. L." Warner is born in 1892:
https://www.masonrytoday.com/index.php?new_month=8&new_day=2&new_year=2016

*

Jack Warner / Famous Freemasons. La Porte York Rite:
https://www.laporteyorkrite.com/famous-masons/name/jack-warner/

JOHN WAYNE

An American Freemason - John Wayne. Northern Masonic Jurisdiction Scottish Rite.

https://scottishritenmj.org/blog/freemason-john-wayne

*

Le petit dictionnaire des (vrais et faux) frères. Alain Bauer, Roger Dachez. Flammarion, pp. 192-193.

*

Masonic biography on the Grand Lodge of British Columbia and Yukon website:
https://freemasonry.bcy.ca/biography/wayne_j/wayne_j.html

COLONEL SANDERS

Colonel Sanders' bio on the official website of the Grand Lodge of Ohio:
https://www.freemason.com/colonel-sanders/

*

Masonic biography on the Grand Lodge of British Columbia and Yukon website:
https://freemasonry.bcy.ca/biography/sanders_h/sanders_h.html

COUNT BASIE

Count Basie - bio on the official website of the Grand Lodge of Ohio:
Musical Masons: The Freemasons of jazz: https://www.freemason.com/freemasons-jazz/

*

The secret history of the jazz greats who were freemasons, John Lewis, The Guardian, 2 lipca 2016: https://www.theguardian.com/music/2014/jul/02/secret-jazz-freemason-history-duke-ellington-sun-ra

MARC CHAGALL

Chagall et la Franc Maçonnerie ou un peintre Maçon très discret. (Chagall and Freemasonry or a very discreet painter Mason) Dominique Beaune, L'edifice. https://www.ledifice.net/7035-K.html

*

La franc-maçonnerie et les peintres, La peinture, outil de perception du monde. Pascal Bajou: http://expositions.bnf.fr/franc-maconnerie/arret/04-3.htm_

*

Les Francs-maçons russes au xxe siècle. Nina Berberova, Actes Sud, Arles, 1990, p. 113.

*

Marc Chagall : Voyager dans la Bible. Published July 4 lipca, 2022 in 'Franc-Maconnerie'.
https://www.fm-mag.fr/article/culture/marc-chagall-voyager-dans-la-bible-2364

SUGAR RAY ROBINSON

Sugar Ray Robinson (Posted 3/8/2015). Ancient Accepted Scottish Rite, Valley of Boston:
https://scottishriteboston.org/en/article_view.php?news_id=595#.ZAOSGHbMKbh

*

Masonic biography on the official website of the mixed Freemasonry Le Droit Humain:
https://www.universalfreemasonry.org/en/famous-freemasons/sugar-ray-robinson

IRVING BERLIN

Irvin Berlin - Masonic biography on the official website of the Grand Lodge of Ohio: Musical Masons:
https://www.freemason.com/irving-berlin/

*

10,000 Famous Freemasons by William R.Denslow, Published by Macoy Publishing & Masonic Supply Co.,
Inc. Richmond, Virginia, 1957.

GERALD FORD

Gerald R.Ford. Valley of Kansas City. Scottish Rite History: https://www.srkc.org/history/famous/ford/

*

Le petit dictionnaire des (vrais et faux) frères. Alain Bauer, Roger Dachez. Flammarion, p. 169.

JOHN GLENN

Grand Lodge of Ohio: Senator, Astronaut. Ohio Freemason. The life of the Illustrious John Glenn, 33°
(Masonic biography on the official website of the Grand Lodge of Ohio): https://www.freemason.com/
john-glenn/

*

Northern Masonic Jurisdiction Scottish Rite: Among the Stars: Freemason Astronuts, October 8, 2020:
https://scottishritenmj.org/blog/masonic-astronauts

HOW TO BECOME
A FREEMASON?

The absolute minimum requirement of any body of Freemasons is that the candidate must be free, and considered to be of good character. There is usually an age requirement, varying greatly between Grand Lodges, and (in some jurisdictions) capable of being overridden by a dispensation from the Grand Lodge. The underlying assumption is that the candidate should be a mature adult.

Additionally, most Grand Lodges require the candidate to declare a belief in a Supreme Being. In a few cases, the candidate may be required to be of a specific religion. The form of Freemasonry most common in Scandinavia (known as the Swedish Rite), for example, accepts only Christians. At the other end of the spectrum, "Liberal" or Continental Freemasonry, exemplified by the Grand Orient de France, does not require a declaration of belief in any deity, and accepts atheists (a cause of discord with the rest of Freemasonry).

(the source/read more: https://en.wikipedia.org/wiki/Masonic_lodge)

To learn more about the requirements for joining Freemasonry, as well as to learn about the many useful tips for any candidate, please visit

https://freemasonry.network/how-to-join/

Written by one of the highest Masonic dignitaries, this unique book reveals the secrets of Freemasonry in inspiring images and quotes. This is probably the largest anthology of its kind (in fact it's over 555 black and white illustrations), enriched with several hundred quotations on the essence of Freemasonry.

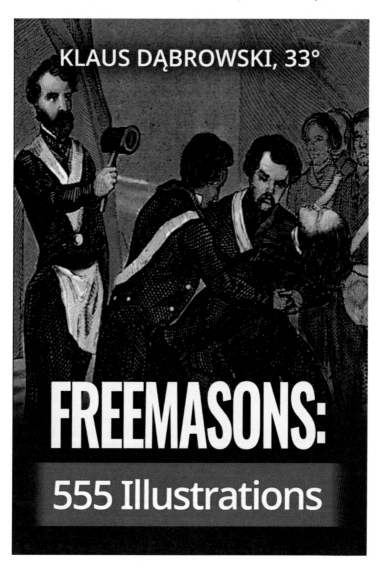

KLAUS DĄBROWSKI, 33°

FREEMASONS:

555 Illustrations

https://freemasonry.network/555-illustrations/

.

Made in the USA
Monee, IL
29 November 2024

71627353R00145